Prostitution, Politics an

C000109674

Prostitution has become an extremely topical issue in recent years and attention has focused both on the situation of female prostitutes and the adequacy of existing forms of regulation. *Prostitution, Politics & Policy* brings together the main debates and issues associated with prostitution in order to examine the range of policy options that are available.

Governments in different parts of the world have been struggling to develop constructive policies to deal with prostitution – as, for example, the British Home Office recently instigated a £1.5 million programme to help address the perceived problems of prostitution. In the context of this struggle, and amidst the publication of various policy documents, *Prostitution, Politics & Policy* develops a fresh approach to understanding this issue, while presenting a range of what are seen as progressive and radical policy proposals. Much of the debate around prostitution has been polarised between liberals – who want prostitution decriminalised, normalised and humanised – and conservatives – who have argued that prostitution should be abolished. But, drawing on a wide range of international literature, and providing an overview that is both accessible to students and relevant to policy makers and practitioners, in this book Roger Matthews proposes a form of radical realism that is irreducible to either of these two positions.

Roger Matthews is Professor of Criminology at London South Bank University.

Prostitution, Politics and Policy

Roger Matthews

Routledge·Cavendish
Taylor & Francis Group
a GlassHouse book

Published 2008 by Routledge-Cavendish
2 Park Square, Milton Park, Abingdon, Oxon OX14 4RN

Simultaneously published in the USA and Canada
by Routledge-Cavendish
270 Madison Ave, New York, NY 10016

*Routledge-Cavendish is an imprint of the Taylor & Francis Group,
an informa business*

© 2008 Roger Matthews

A GlassHouse book

Typeset in Times by
RefineCatch Limited, Bungay, Suffolk
Printed and bound in Great Britain by
TJ International Ltd, Padstow, Cornwall

British Library Cataloguing in Publication Data
A catalogue record for this book is available from the British Library

Library of Congress Cataloging-in-Publication Data
Matthews, Roger, 1948–
   Prostitution, politics & policy / Roger Matthews.
     p. cm.
   Includes bibliographical references.
   1. Prostitution.   2. Prostitution—Government
policy.   3. Prostitution—Political aspects.   I. Title.
   HQ118.M38 2008
   363.4′4—dc22

                        2007039652

ISBN 978–0–415–45916–7 (hbk)
     978–0–415–45917–4 (pbk)
     978–0–203–93087–8 (e-book)

Contents

Preface

This book is the culmination of over 20 years research and writing on different aspects of prostitution. Over this period the nature of prostitution and the associated debates have changed significantly. In the UK there was a limited interest in this issue until the late 1980s when prostitution was identified as a source of HIV transmission. Over the last two decades, however, the issue of prostitution has risen up the social and political agenda. The first chapter of this book outlines the main developments which have occurred nationally and internationally and have thereby influenced how the issue has been conceived and responded to.

Although this book was planned long before the five women who were involved in street prostitution in Ipswich – Paula Clennell, Annette Nichols, Anneli Alderton, Gemma Adams and Tania Nicol – were murdered in December 2006, its orientation and emphasis has been deeply influenced by these events. It is not only the tragic nature of these murders, which brought home so acutely the extreme vulnerability of the women involved, but the fact that some women kept on working although they were aware that a murderer was targeting working women in the area. Of particular significance was that one of the women, Paula Clennell, who was interviewed by television journalists after the first murder and said that although she was going to try to take precautions she felt that she had to continue working to finance her drug habit. A few days later she was also found dead. The response of the police and other agencies that advised the women to keep off the streets has subsequently been recognised by those involved as inadequate. The relevant agencies adopting a standard harm reduction model failed to provide the necessary resources, accommodation, treatment and support which would have allowed these women to stop working, at least until the murderer was caught. The 30 or so women who were involved in street prostitution in Ipswich were only encouraged to leave the streets temporarily as a result of financial support given by an unnamed charity according to newspaper reports.

The response by the relevant agencies in this situation, however, underlined the limitations of current policies that allow women to continue working in this dangerous environment with limited protection and support. It also raised questions about the viability of established responses to street prostitution and indicated that a more proactive approach may be necessary.

The public response and media reporting of the murders in Ipswich appear, however, to represent something of a watershed in attitudes towards women involved in street prostitution. Compared to the ways in which the victims were reported in the 'Yorkshire Ripper' case some 30 years before, there was noticeably more public sympathy for the plight of these women and a greater sensitivity in reporting. There was a debate in national newspapers about the use of key terms and whether the term 'prostitute' was appropriate and indeed whether the women concerned should be referred to as 'prostitutes' at all. In the policy debate that ensued there was a widespread consensus that the women working on the streets of Ipswich and elsewhere should be seen as victims rather than offenders in need of support rather than punishment. These discussions and debates in the public sphere more or less directly suggested that a radical and comprehensive approach to street prostitution needs to be developed and that current policies require a thorough review.

Thus the primary focus of this book is female street prostitution. Research and knowledge about off-street prostitution in the UK and elsewhere remains very patchy. Therefore there is always a possibility that understandings based on research on street prostitution are generalised to all those women involved in all forms of prostitution. A corollary to the tendency to generalise from street prostitution to prostitution in general is the belief that while street prostitution may be associated with a range of problems both for individual women and communities, that off-street prostitution is relatively problem free. Although the existing research is sparse the evidence suggests that off-street prostitution involves a number of specific issues and is far from problem free. Where possible, reference will be made to the available evidence on off-street prostitution which, whilst not comprehensive, is sufficient to qualify any claims that the resolution to the issue of prostitution is to reduce or remove the street trade while allowing the off-street trade to flourish. Also, the book does not directly engage with issues associated with male homosexual prostitution. Although there are points of overlap between male homosexual and female heterosexual prostitution the former has a set of unique attributes and dynamics that need to be addressed separately.

Finally, the book does not engage directly with the wide-ranging feminist literature that has brought a welcome theoretical and political dimension to the debate. This literature, however, provides an important backdrop to the issues covered. The feminist debate, however, is characterised by a deep division between liberal feminists, on the one hand, who want to normalise prostitution and see it as a legitimate form of work and the radical feminists on the other who claim that prostitution involves violence against women. From the vantage point of a middle-aged male the aim of this book is to try to steer a path through these two opposed positions and to develop a theoretical and policy response to prostitution which is both critical and realist. This book however is not an attempt at pure synthesis or compromise. Rather, it aims to develop an approach that avoids some of the extremes of the current debate, while being critical of the liberal and conservative positions that currently dominate the debate in the UK and other countries.

Roger Matthews
September 2007

Table of legislation

Chapter 1

Why has prostitution become an issue?

Introduction

Prostitution has until recently been an 'invisible' issue. Despite the many thousands of women involved in the sale of sexual services, and even greater numbers of men who purchase these services, research and publications on prostitution for much of the post-war period has been relatively limited. For most of this period the street trade has been largely confined to cert-in red light districts and therefore out of sight to the general public. Consequently, from the 1950s to the 1980s there has been relatively little public or political concern focused on prostitution and its regulation remains largely based on reducing the visibility of prostitution and confining it to certain locations.

The focus of attention has been mainly directed at the women involved in prostitution and at street prostitution rather than the off-street trade. In many countries, including the UK there has until recently been very little interest in male clients. However, in England and Wales legislation was introduced in the 1980s to address what was seen as the increasing problem of kerb crawling, while in the same decade the sanction of imprisonment was removed for soliciting related offences (see Benson and Matthews 1996; Self 2003). A limited number of Private Members Bills were tabled between the 1960s and the mid 1980s, but the issue of prostitution remained relatively muted, except when it involved high-profile celebrities and politicians (Denning 1993).

However, in the late 1980s prostitution came increasingly to the forefront of public attention and moved up the social and political agenda in different countries around the world including most European countries, America, Canada and Australia. A number of factors contributed to the change of interest. These included the growing concerns about the spread of HIV/AIDS, the growth of prostitute support and campaigning groups, increased public demands to control street prostitution, the declaration of the 'war on drugs', the growing preoccupation with trafficking and the visible increase in the number of foreign women involved in prostitution as well as greater concern for children involved in prostitution. Underpinning many of these developments has been a growing feminist interest in this issue, which has become manifested in a number of lively, and at times, heated debates among feminists of different persuasions (Ericsson 1980; Jaget 1980; Millett 1975; Nagle 1997; O'Neill 2001).

The HIV/AIDS panic

Whereas in the 1960s and 1970s prostitution in the UK had largely been conceived a problem of public order, during the 1980s it increasingly became seen as a medical issue linked to the growing concerns about the spread of HIV/AIDS. In many respects, the shift towards the medicalisation of prostitution in this period was reminiscent of the nineteenth century debates about the spread of syphilis and other sexually transmitted diseases (Rosenberg 1988; Walkowitz 1980). As the panic about the spread of HIV/AIDS intensified during the 1980s, prostitutes were quickly identified as a potential 'vehicle' of transmission between marginalised populations and respectable society. Many policy makers saw prostitution as a potential 'bridge' between the underclass and mainstream society. As in the nineteenth century, images of dirt, disease and contagion abounded and the prostitute, through her acknowledged promiscuity, was seen as a likely carrier of contagion (Corbin 1990).

The fears about the spread of HIV/AIDS were intensified by the knowledge that there was no known cure, and claims in the media that the spread of HIV/AIDS could be more devastating than the Black Death heightened anxieties. Moreover, the increasing mobilisation of powerful medical metaphors of contagion and invasion justified the introduction of urgent and severe measures to halt the spread of the disease. Increasingly, HIV/AIDS was associated with evil and was seen to infect the body but also to exploit social vulnerabilities. As Susan Sontag (1983) has argued, the sexual transmission of this illness was considered by most people as a calamity one brings on oneself and increasingly AIDS became seen not only as a disease of sexual excess but of perversity.

Not surprisingly, the public and policy makers focused attention on the prostitute who was increasingly constructed as an object for medical investigation. Research agencies and a new body of experts emerged to soak up the funding that was being directed at the issue. Research funding, which had been conspicuously absent in previous decades, suddenly became widely available to those who were prepared to try to limit the possibilities of contamination via commercialised sexual activity, by focusing on those who were seen as potentially one of the main 'carriers' of the disease – the prostitute.

However, after a number of years of panic it became increasingly evident that female prostitutes had, in general, a relatively low level of HIV, unless they happened to be intravenous drug users. Research increasingly revealed that the spread of HIV/AIDS was largely concentrated amongst intravenous drug users and homosexual men, despite the repeated warnings that it would soon spread to the general population. It also became apparent in those female prostitutes who did contract HIV, that the most likely source of infection was the woman's husband or boyfriend (Darrow 1990). By the early 1990s policy makers in Europe and America cautiously concluded that prostitution played no major part in the spread of HIV, although the emphasis on the need to practice 'safe sex' remained in force. By this time the distribution of condoms and lubricants by the newly established support agencies had become well established as part of a harm minimisation strategy.

In a period in which concerns about the possible transmission of HIV/AIDS were focused on prostitution it might have been expected that the dominant policy position would have been to try to reduce the number of people involved in prostitution. But many of the newly established agencies, which had been specifically set up to support and monitor prostitutes were not particularly interested in discouraging clients in this way. Rather, they argued that funding should be maintained, if not increased, and although they conceded that female prostitutes posed little risk in relation to HIV transmission, they warned that without continued vigilance there was a real danger that HIV could affect both prostitutes and their clients.

This ambivalent position is expressed by one of the leading researchers and commentators on the subject. He states:

> (As noted earlier), it is unrealistic and would probably be counterproductive to attempt to discourage, reduce or even ban prostitution. Such a policy would have adverse effects for AIDS prevention, since it would inevitably deter people from seeking proper health care. Measures are needed to greatly increase contacts between prostitutes, their clients and health services. People should be encouraged to seek regular check-ups with the guarantee of a 'user friendly' confidential service. In areas in which prostitution is extensive, specialist health workers should be appointed who should if necessary seek out prostitutes to enlist their participation in health checks and AIDS prevention activities.
>
> (Plant 1990: 202)

Martin Plant spoke on behalf of many of the newly arrived quasi-medical agencies who wanted to maintain a well resourced but more sanitised trade in sexual services. These agencies wanted to continue to supply condoms and lubricants as well as give advice, rather than contemplate the reduction of the number of women involved in prostitution and thereby reducing the overall number of commercial sexual encounters.

There was, of course, no formal contradiction between the objectives of reducing the scale of prostitution and finding ways of encouraging women to practice safer sex. The argument that developing measures to discourage or reduce prostitution would in some way undermine the provision of health services is disingenuous and suggests that the main interest of these newly formed health agencies was to maintain a manageable, dependent and accessible clientele. There was little or no interest in addressing the often oppressive, coercive or exploitative situation in which many of their 'clients' operated.

It largely escaped the attention of these agencies and their funders that the focus was primarily on the female prostitutes while their male clients went largely unchecked. The ideology that the disease resided in the female body was sustained and the female prostitute continued to be seen as the 'carrier' of disease. This in turn fuelled the conception of prostitutes as impure and disease-ridden.

As it became increasingly evident that female prostitutes had a relatively low level of HIV infection and the HIV/AIDS panic gradually subsided in the early 1990s, the funding for these health agencies decreased. Consequently, many redefined their role and objectives. Increasingly, they began providing a different range of services and acted as representatives of female prostitutes and in doing so they rejected abolitionism and regulationism and advocated a more liberal harm reduction approach (Ward and Day 1997). Their work inspired the creation of a number of agencies providing healthcare, advice, outreach work, drop-in centres and other services for women involved in prostitution with the consequence that by the end of the 1990s over 100 agencies had been set up in the UK with nearly all urban centres having at least one specialist agency.

The growth of prostitute support and campaigning groups

During the 1970s and 1980s a number of groups emerged in Europe and America to represent and promote the rights of prostitutes. Some of these groups like COYOTE (Call of Your Old Tired Ethics) in America and the ECP (English Collective of Prostitutes) in the UK advocated the decriminal- isation and normalisation of prostitution. That is, they set out to counter the stigmatisation, which was directed at women involved in prostitution and to challenge some of the popular stereotypes of the prostitute. They oppose in general any form of state interference in the operation of the sex market arguing that the state should not be involved in the legislation of morality (ECP 2004; Jenness 1990).

Although these and similar groups in other countries claim to include and represent prostitutes, the involvement of active prostitutes is very limited. One survey for example, found that approximately 3 per cent COYOTE's members were practising prostitutes (Weitzer 2000). Interviews with active prostitutes in the UK in the mid 1980s found that the overwhelming majority of women working on the streets in London had not heard of the ECP and were not aware of the policies that they advocated (Matthews 1986a). A local survey carried out at that time with women involved in street prostitution found that approximately a quarter supported decriminalisation while almost three quarters advocated some form of state regulation (Dunn 1984).

The lack of participation of working women, however, has not detracted from the impact and publicity which these groups were able to mobilise. Through a stream of publications, radio and television appearances and exposure through other media they provide a critical opposition to government policy and regularly contributed to public and political debates on the subject.

In the Netherlands organisations such as 'Red Thread' (Rode Draad) have similarly been influential in challenging Dutch policy on prostitution, arguing that prostitution is a profession and should be dealt with pragmatically by the government. Its main concerns are the rights and working conditions of women involved in prostitution and campaigning for the decriminalisation of prostitution; although it appears to give some support to the policy of legalisation, which has been recently introduced in the Netherlands. Other European countries have national agencies that actively attempt to promote what they see as the best interest of those involved in prostitution. There are also pan-European agencies such as EUROPAP (European Network for HIV-STD Prevention in Prostitution), which as the name suggests is primarily concerned with health issues. It is interesting to note, in passing, that these relatively long standing organisations that advocate the normalisation and de-stigmatisation of prostitution still use the term 'prostitute' rather than 'sex worker'. The term 'sex worker' did not become common currency until the 1990s with the establishment of a growing number of locally based agencies.

The development of locally based agencies providing a range of support and outreach work mainly for those involved in street prostitution has changed the political and organisational framework of prostitution in the UK. In contrast to the national organisations, they tend to be more 'hands on'. Working in specific localities with identifiable 'clients' and increasingly in conjunction with a range of other agencies, including community representatives, these agencies are more ingrained in local politics. They advocate a predominantly 'non-judgemental' approach and are involved on a daily basis in the politics of prostitution and therefore have to exercise some flexibility in terms of both policy and practice.

In the UK these different local 'sex work' projects have organised themselves into the United Kingdom Network of Sex Work Projects (UKNSWP), which currently represents 79 projects. Its role is to coordinate activities of the various local projects and to campaign on their behalf at a national level. Recently, the UKNSWP engaged in a campaign to introduce 'toleration zones' in England and Wales and this option forms one of the main planks of its policy programme (Van Doorninck and Campbell 2006).

One of the most high profile campaigns, which the UKNSWP and other prostitute-orientated groups have mounted, has been the reduction of violence from clients. Although the issue of violence has been mainly client centred with only passing reference to the violence that those involved in prostitution experience at the hands of pimps or partners, campaigns such as the 'ugly mugs' initiative have been mobilised in an attempt to both reduce violence and simultaneously draw attention to the frequent attacks experienced by women working on the street.

The 'ugly mugs' and similar campaigns, which have circulated details of known offenders, have sensitised both the public and the police who are now under increasing pressure to take reports of violence against women involved in prostitution seriously. The increased concern with violence against street prostitutes, however, has had a number of consequences. First, it has increasingly identified the prostitute as a victim. Second, it has probably deterred many would-be prostitutes from engaging in prostitution or alternatively encouraged those involved in street prostitution to leave 'the game'. Third, it has almost certainly led to greater public awareness of the association between violence and street prostitution and made some residents more reluctant to accommodate prostitution in their neighbourhoods.

How influential these local and national support groups have been in influencing social attitudes and policy making is difficult to estimate, but there is little doubt at the local level the growing number of prostitutes support agencies has profoundly altered the political complexion in many areas of the UK. This has resulted in new forms of governance and modes of regulation (Scoular and O'Neill 2007). They have probably been most influential in mobilising sympathy and understanding for the prostitute amongst local agencies and served to present a more positive image of those involved in prostitution. Working with the police and other agencies they have advocated non-enforcement policies and the impact of this strategy is reflected in the substantial decrease in the number of female prostitutes arrested in England and Wales over the past decade for soliciting (Matthews 2005).

One of the primary objectives of the increasingly influential prostitute support groups has been to try to promote the rights of female prostitutes. However, Julia O'Connell Davidson (1998) has argued that the specific power relations between the prostitute and the client provide a fundamental obstacle to the achievement of prostitute's rights. She maintains that the power and economic differentials in play ensures that prostitutes are subject to economic compulsion even when they are formally 'free'. Thus, for O'Connell Davidson, prostitutes organisations are limited in what they can achieve, partly because they fail to fully understand the economics of prostitution and also because of the predominantly liberal stance adopted by these groups.

While O'Connell Davidson's point about the analytic and political limitations of the various groupings that have emerged in recent years to promote the rights and well-being of prostitutes has some merit, her conclusion is, as Jackie West (2000) has argued, unduly pessimistic. Although these groups and agencies may have been more effective at the local rather than at the national level they have been influential in shaping perceptions of the prostitute, if not in changing policies on prostitution. West sees the limitations of these activist groups stemming from the limited participation of working women, on one hand, and the failure of these groups to develop effective alliances with other organisations, on the other. However, she does concede that prostitute activists have been an effective voice of dissent in challenging the current legislation and in placing both licensing and decriminalisation on the agenda in different countries. There has also been a movement to 'professionalise' prostitution through the establishment of unions and the provision of occupational advice (Lopes 2006).

The community response

One of the most significant developments during the 1980s in Britain and elsewhere has been the changing public response to prostitution, particularly among those who live in red light districts (Allwood 2004; Brock 1998). Neighbourhood protests emerged during the 1980s and 1990s in Southampton, Sheffield, Stoke, Birmingham, Bradford, Glasgow, Leeds, Liverpool, Walsall, Cardiff and various parts of London. Urban areas in which prostitution had been practised for many years became sites of confrontation and agitation. Local residents up and down the country, who for many years had tolerated street prostitution, began to campaign for the removal of prostitution from 'their' neighbourhoods. The reasons for this change in the nature of public attitudes varied between different locations. In some areas, it was linked to noise and nuisance, with residents bitterly complaining of finding used condoms and other paraphernalia on their doorsteps and gardens, while others objected to the increasing number of cars which routinely cruised around red light districts and the frequent arguments on the streets between prostitutes, clients and pimps (O'Neill and Campbell 2004; Matthews 1986a; 1992).

The second factor centred around notions of personal security and freedom of movement in those areas in which these issues were coming to the fore. Feminists, in particular, had drawn attention to the fact that many women living in inner city areas operated under an unofficial curfew and did not feel safe going out alone at night. For women living in and around the red light districts these concerns were compounded and there were reports from the women living in these areas of being regularly propositioned, harassed and, on some occasions, assaulted.

Closely related to the issues of personal security and freedom of movement was a changing sense of disorder. This change has been gradual and difficult to quantify, but the growing objection to vagrancy, street begging and young people 'hanging around' reflect a change of public sensibilities. The changing concerns with security have also been reflected in the growth of gated communities and the introduction of security systems on council housing estates. The changing sense of space involved new notions of 'ownership', which in many areas became linked with new forms of privatisation, as neighbourhoods became more fragmented. This change was, in turn, linked to the changing nature of communities (Young 2001).

Significantly, however, the growing concerns with the impact of street prostitution on community life served to galvanise a number of different residents' groups. Street prostitution became *the* major issue of public concern in certain locations. Public meetings in affected areas were often packed and emotions ran high. In most of these meetings, which tended to be organised by the local authorities, residents' groups demanded that something be done. In some areas, such as Birmingham and Streatham in South London, where the police and other authorities were seen to be unresponsive, residents set up street patrols and in some cases vigilante groups (Sagar 2005). There are issues about accountability, representativeness and the methods used by some of these residents' groups. However, the formation of street patrols was an expression of the growing frustration with official bodies that were seen not to take the issue seriously.

Related to the increased demand for service and protection from the authorities was a growing sense of empowerment by some local residents' groups who saw themselves as consumers and citizens who were paying for security and who now demanded a certain quality of life. Thus, they had few reservations in calling on local authorities, the police, and other bodies to address the issue of street prostitution. In some areas, the changing attitudes towards street prostitution were bound up with a process of gentrification. In places where poor and deprived areas had been regenerated through urban development grants a change of class composition affected a change of local politics. For while disempowered poorer residents who often lacked organisation and political clout had for many years put up with street prostitution in their neighbourhood, the residents in these gentrified or regenerated areas were no longer prepared to tolerate this situation. In addition, they were more organised and articulate and in some areas were able to effectively close down or displace street prostitution in a relatively short period of time (Hubbard 2004).

The final factor that was in play during this period was a change in moral and religious attitudes. In some communities, the visibility of women parading themselves on the streets and selling sexual services was deemed unacceptable. In Muslim communities in the Midlands, for example, local residents stood outside their own doorways in order to deter prostitutes (Hubbard 1998). Approximately 150 residents in Balsall Heath in Birmingham turned out each night at the height of the campaign to take down registration numbers of kerb crawlers. One report summarises these issues:

> Two years ago, Balsall Heath in Birmingham was the hub of a £10 million a year prostitution business. 450 girls plied its pavements attracting hundreds of kerb crawlers. Pimps and drug dealers lurked around. Local residents were afraid to walk the streets and unable to sleep at night because of the noise. Today the problem has been all but eradicated. Only 5 prostitutes are left, the pimps and drug dealers have disappeared and all

types of crime have stopped. Using three mobile phones and a porter cabin, local volunteers have solved a problem which the police, spending £500,000 a year were unable to dent.

(Lean 2003:1)

Some commentators have raised the issue of displacement in relation to interventions of this type (Lowman 1992; Hubbard 1998). Displacement is always a possible effect of any street based intervention but the level of displacement is in the majority of cases only a proportion of the original problem and even when displacement does occur it can be benign (Barr and Pease 1990). In cases, for example, where street prostitution is displaced away from residential areas to parks or industrial areas, it is widely seen as benign displacement.

Research which was carried out in relation to a community-driven multi-agency initiative in Finsbury Park in North London found that over a period of two years the vast majority of the 250 women who were actively involved in street prostitution in 1986 left prostitution; leaving a 'hard core' of mostly older women working from a local public house (Matthews 1986a). A search of names and addresses which was carried out a few years later revealed that very few of these women had moved to other parts of London or other parts of the country to engage in prostitution (Matthews 1992). The same study also showed that rather than wholesale displacement taking place that there was a 'diffusion of benefits' and that other forms of victimisation in the area decreased (Clarke and Weisburd 1994)

A number of forces combined in different ways in different areas to decrease public tolerance of street prostitution and to mobilise both formal and informal responses to reduce its visibility, impact and scale. Increasing pressure was brought to bear on the police and local authorities to 'do something' about this problem and to help residents 'win back' local streets and neighbourhoods. This was predominantly a bottom-up community-based offensive involving a number of like-minded but independent groups in different parts of the country. The mobilisation of local residents around this issue seemed to increase the confidence of the residents and was a source of empowerment for these groups. In many cases, but not all, residents' groups were effective in reducing the level and impact of street prostitution and in some areas they have subsequently turned their attention to other issues of crime and disorder (Matthews and Pitts 2001).

Significantly, in the debates that ensued the majority of residents were opposed to prostitution and not the prostitutes. For the most part, residents saw the women working on the street as unfortunates. Their problematic drug use, poor health and physical condition, as well as visible evidence of the women being the victims of violence from pimps and punters, elicited sympathy rather than anger. Their hostility, however, increasingly turned towards the male clients, either because it became evident that many of those cruising around the streets were voyeurs and were attracted to red light districts as sites of entertainment, or alternatively were the persistent and sometimes aggressive punters who intimidated local women and created a sense of disorder and a lack of control.

Ron Weitzer (1994) has described similar processes in America in which anti-prostitution neighbourhood groups have engaged in campaigns in cities across the US. Frustrated with the police and other officials they have taken direct action to reduce or remove street prostitution from their neighbourhoods. As in the UK, American residents groups have set up street patrols and have also turned their attention increasingly to the customers. The international nature of what might be described as an anti-street prostitution movement suggests that it is not reducible to changing religious beliefs or class compositions of neighbourhoods, gentrification or simply a consequence of residents becoming increasingly intolerant. Rather the increasing groundswell of opposition against street prostitution in a number of different countries simultaneously appears to be bound up with the more fundamental changes of the dynamics of the urban life in late modernity.

In sum, the increased mobilisation of residents groups in different urban centres has made the ability of prostitutes and clients to operate increasingly difficult. This had the effect of deterring the number of would-be clients in many areas and encouraged women involved in street prostitution either to move to unfamiliar locations or to leave prostitution. There is some evidence that in some of these areas the more casual of 'amateur' women who in previous periods became involved in prostitution to pay off debts or to meet bills have been increasingly deterred, while others may have left prostitution earlier than they otherwise would have done (Matthews 1986a). Thus, the widespread mobilisation of local community groups appears to have the dual effect of politicising the issue of street prostitution, on one hand, while reducing the scale and visibility of street prostitution on the other.

Prostitution and the 'war on drugs'

Just at the point when the battle against HIV/AIDS looked like it was being won in Europe and America, a new and more enduring quasi-medical offensive began to gain momentum. Dubbed the 'war on drugs', a major offensive was developed to tackle what was perceived to be the growing problem of drug use, although the 'war' tended to be waged predominantly at certain types of drugs and certain groups of people.

Those most directly in the firing line were poorer and marginalised populations whose drug of choice was heroin or crack cocaine (Tonry 1995). Street prostitution became an obvious target for the anti-drugs offensive and the reports that between 50 to 90 per cent of street prostitutes in the UK were drug addicted fuelled these concerns. A series of research studies reported the high levels of drug use among those involved in prostitution and increasingly the entry, continuing involvement and the difficulties of leaving prostitution became seen as a function of problematic drug use (Church et al. 2001; Hester and Westmarland 2004; Mckegany and Barnard 1996; Pitcher and Aris 2003).

This development had the effect of obscuring the aetiology of prostitution by transforming it from an essentially economic issue to a problem of drug abuse. Popular and official depictions of the female prostitute increasingly presented her as someone who had entered prostitution to earn the money to sustain an expensive drugs habit. Indeed, during the 1990s this became one of the predominant explanations of why women came to engage in prostitution (Hunter and May 2004).

As with all ideologies, the increasing preoccupation with drug abuse in relation to prostitution had a rational core. The studies which were conducted no doubt represented a change in reality, with a growing percentage of those involved in street prostitution using or misusing crack cocaine and heroin. However, these snapshot surveys tended to overlook the processes which produced this new reality and the changing image of the drug-ridden street prostitute.

As some commentators have pointed out, heavy drug use has historically been linked to prostitution and is generally seen as a coping mechanism for dealing with the pressures and strains arising from involvement in this activity. Consistent drug use, particularly in the form of alcohol, has been widely reported in interviews with those involved in prostitution prior to the 1990s. The main change that seems to have taken place is a change in the type of drug use with crack cocaine, which is highly addictive, becoming more widely used among street prostitutes. But in certain parts of the UK, it is not only the drug of choice that has changed, but also a change in the composition of street prostitution. As the numbers involved in street prostitution have declined in a number of urban centres a significant number of the more sporadic 'amateur' women who in the past turned to prostitution in times of financial crisis are less evident, either as a result of growing fears of violence or the growing pressure from residents and the police. The decline in the numbers of what we might call 'economic' prostitutes means that a growing proportion of those left working on the streets are more disorganised, marginalised, desperate and in the majority of cases drug dependent. Thus, the composition of street prostitution has changed and those that remain are less able and less willing to conceal their drug addiction.

In the UK the number of cocaine users is reported to have increased rapidly in the 1990s and it was estimated that in the period 1988–89 to 2002–03, crack cocaine accounted for 6 per cent of drug offences in the London area (GLADA 2004). But it was crack cocaine, used predominantly by the poor and the marginalised rather than powder cocaine, which is the drug of choice amongst the more affluent sections of the middle class, that became the primary target of intervention. It was, however, crack cocaine that tended to be singled out for attention within a growing culture of poly-drug use. (Parker et al. 1998).

The growing body of research, which detailed the overlap between drug markets and sex markets, reinforced the association between drug use and prostitution (May et al. 1999; Hunter and May 2004). Moreover, some of those who had been involved in researching the relationship between HIV and prostitution later became involved in documenting the links between drugs and prostitution (Plant 1997). Although the literature points to the personal and social proximity of drug use and prostitution, the causal relationship between the two tends to be assumed rather than demonstrated (May and Hunter 2006).

There can be little doubt that a large percentage of street prostitutes in the UK are using heroin or crack cocaine, but the complex relation between involvement in prostitution and drug use remains unclear. It may well be the case that many of these women would be problem drug users whether they were involved in prostitution or not, and vice versa.

Moreover, the finding that sex markets are located close to drug markets is hardly surprising. Both types of markets require a consistent throughput of populations and a low level of organised public opposition. Main thoroughfares and transport hubs in transient areas are typically the areas favoured by both markets. Thus in reality, the impact of closing down drug markets on the operation of sex markets is likely to be limited since the relation between the two markets is more contingent than causal. Also, in terms of aetiology, research indicates that those who work off-street are not so frequently associated with problem drug use. The concentration of policy and research on street prostitution has tended to overstate the role of drugs, particularly heroin and crack cocaine, in the operation of prostitution as a whole (Church et al. 2001). In the UK the off street trade has been the fastest growing sector of the sex industry and many of the brothels and escort agencies will not employ those who show signs of problematic drug use.

By the early 1990s the association between problem drug use and prostitution had been firmly established in America. Over two thirds of female prostitutes in one national study were found to be using heroin or cocaine, while almost a third were using crack cocaine (Sterk and Elifson 1990). The rise of crack cocaine, in particular, was linked with increased violence, instability and anxiety. Heavy drug use was also linked to the increased victimisation of women involved in prostitution, since it was claimed that they tended to lose control, on one hand, and become more vulnerable, on the other.

Trafficking and migration

The growing visibility of foreign women working as prostitutes in different countries has resonated with changing social and political concerns (Kantola and Squires 2004). In general, the movement of women across borders to engage in prostitution is increasingly bound up with the growing international concerns about immigration, whether it is legal or not, as well as issues of multi-culturalism, the changing nature of communities, globalisation, organised crime and growing fears about national security (Goodey, 2003; Outshoorn 2004). The internationalisation of the sex trade has also become increasingly associated with the different forms of 'border crossing' linking geographical, social and personal forms of transgression (Young 2007).

Those who are coerced or abducted are seen as victims, while others are seen as offenders. The recurring horror stories of coercion, abuse, and deception, as well as the role of international criminal networks in orchestrating this trade represents, in the eyes of many observers, the downside of increased migration and globalisation. One report in *The Economist*, for example, captured this response when it suggested that in the UK:

> Such disregard for national borders is characteristic of the sex industry. Having turned a profit more quickly then almost any other enterprise, it is now in the vanguard of globalisation. For prostitutes and those who make money from them, the advantages of migration and free labour are clear: wage differentials are high, English-speaking skills are not essential, and because the whole sector is unregulated, there are no trade unions or protectionist labour laws to worry about.
>
> (*The Economist*, 2 September 2004)

The article notes that the while the level of sex trafficking into the UK appears to have significantly increased over the last decade, over the same period the level of regulation of prostitution in general and brothels in particular has decreased. Other newspaper reports in the UK have emphasised the growing proportion of foreign women involved in prostitution around the country, claiming that in London, for example, between 70–80 per cent of the women working in the brothels are foreign and come mainly from Eastern Europe, South Africa, and South East Asia (Ward and Gillan 2006).

Several organisations, specialist agencies and committees have been established in recent years as the issue of trafficking has moved up the international agenda. The reasons given for the increasing international focus on sexual exploitation are that the 'sex sector' is becoming a significant component of many economies, the increase in the scale and speed of movement of human groups across borders in recent years, the greater economic differentials between rich and poor nations, the global feminisation of poverty, and the increasing involvement of organised crime in the trafficking of persons. There is a widespread belief that the number of women trafficked into the sex industry is growing in the UK and other countries, although it has been found in the UK that police forces have a limited knowledge of and give limited attention to trafficking outside of London. Consequently, rather than actively addressing trafficking, police forces around the country are inadvertently contributing to a culture of toleration in relation to trafficking (Kelly and Regan 2003).

A study produced for the European Parliament in 2005 on Trafficking in Women and Children found that despite the increased formal attention given to this subject in Europe, only one in four member states produce reliable quantitative data on trafficking, and the UK is identified as being amongst those countries that have a low reliability of data. Given the limitations of the data the study reports that in 2000 the number of women and children trafficked in 11 selected EC countries was believed to be between 44,000 and 88,000. By 2002 it was estimated that the numbers had increased by around 20 per cent (Rechard 2005). The number of women and children trafficked into different EU countries according to this study is a function of the levels of unemployment, nature of welfare provision, immigration policies and types of anti-trafficking controls. It is also suggested that the mode of regulation will affect the degree of trafficking as will the balance between street and indoor prostitution.

A central debate that runs through the international literature is the distinction between forced and voluntary forms of migration and by implication the 'victim' status of the women involved. The United Nations Optional Protocol to Prevent, Suppress and Punish the Trafficking in Persons, Especially Women and Children was ratified in 2000. Providing a marked departure from its predecessor, the 1948 Convention on the Suppression of Traffic in Persons and the Exploitation of the Prostitution of Others, it aimed to provide a more effective international response and to reclassify the severity of people smuggling and trafficking offences:

> In particular, there was a shift away from an essentially abolitionist approach to prostitution and a stronger sense of the need to see trafficked persons as victims, with all the attendant rights to assistance and social support which it entails. In addition, there was an explicit grounding of the trafficking offence within the context of transnational organised crime and a concerted effort to clarify the relationship between trafficking and other forms of facilitated illegal migration, such as smuggling. None of the developments thus reflected in the Protocol was uncontroversial, however. Even the suggestion that trafficked persons be seen as victims involved difficult negotiation, not only to who counts as a trafficked person and as to what level of assistance is appropriate, but also as to who is responsible for the provision and financing of this support.
>
> (Monro 2006)

The difficulties of determining the appropriate status and response to those involved in facilitated illegal migration and trafficking is partly conceptual and partly political. This issue is subject to a considerable degree of active lobbying by competing interest groups, particularly in the form of the Global

Alliance Against Trafficking in Women (GATW) and the Coalition Against Trafficking in Women (CATW). Although both groups argue for the provision of services for victims of trafficking and the criminalisation of traffickers they are divided on the question of the status of prostitution. The Global Alliance Against Trafficking in Women sees prostitution as legitimate occupation, and essentially as a form of non-exploitative labour. The Coalition Against Trafficking in Women, on the other hand, sees involvement in prostitution as inherently exploitative and is therefore opposed to all forms of trafficking for sexual purposes, regardless of the level of voluntariness involved.

The recurring theme that runs through these debates and related official publications is the issue of 'consent' and relatedly the definition of 'trafficking'. United Nations and European Union publications on these issues have continually debated the meaning and significance of these key terms and have deliberated at length whether the legislation should be specifically gendered and also whether prostitution should be singled out for special consideration. The inability to satisfactorily resolve these central debates, coupled with the fact that each country has developed its own particular response means that policies are internationally uneven and in some cases inconsistent.

It has been suggested that the terms of the debate need to be rethought and that it might be more appropriate, for example, to consider these issues in terms of exploitation as the defining element of trafficking (Monro 2006). At present, however, policies on trafficking in most countries are caught up in debates about consent and the role of force in the process. Consequently, although there is a considerable degree of sympathy for those who are 'trafficked' and a desire in many countries to see the women involved as 'victims', the current terms of the debate make recognition of victim status difficult. Consequently, many of those women who become involved in prostitution in different countries are treated simply as illegal immigrants and deported, while their illegal status makes them vulnerable to traffickers, exploiters and unscrupulous entrepreneurs.

Child prostitution

During the 1990s the issue of young people involved in prostitution came to the fore, both nationally and internationally. Increasingly, it became recognised that it was adults who often controlled the recruitment of children into prostitution and in many cases benefited from their involvement. The vast majority of clients in these cases were adult men. Campaigns against child prostitution have a long history dating back to the purity movements of the nineteenth century. However, the campaigns which have emerged over the last decade or so provide a different emphasis and impetus from that generated by nineteenth century philanthropists and campaigners and has been influenced by changing conceptions of childhood and victimisation.

In the UK, the Children Act 1989 placed responsibility on local authorities to safeguard and promote the welfare of children. The local authorities under the Act are also charged with protecting children from 'significant harm' and have an obligation to provide accommodation for children in need within their area. In general, it established a framework for responding to children who were involved in prostitution or 'at risk' of being involved in prostitution.

On the international front, the United Nations Convention on the Rights of the Child (1995) established guidelines for the treatment and protection of children. Article 34 specifically concerns itself with child prostitution. It states that all states that have ratified the convention shall:

> Undertake to protect the child from all forms of sexual exploitation and sexual abuse. For these purposes States Parties shall in particular take all appropriate national, bilateral and multilateral measures to prevent a) the inducement or coercion of a child to engage in an unlawful sexual activity; b) the exploitative use of children in prostitution or other unlawful sexual practices; c) the exploitative use of children in pornographic performance and materials.

Other articles in the convention made reference to the prevention of abduction and the sale or trafficking in children for any purpose. The Council of Europe in 1993 in its publications in 'Sexual Exploitation, Pornography and Prostitution' called for a change in attitudes and responses to child prostitution. It recommended that members take a 'victimological approach' seeing those under eighteen as victims of sexual exploitation not as perpetrators of a criminal offence. The Council also advocated an extensive public education programme to increase awareness, both among children and the general public, of the dangers and effects of the sexual exploitation of children. A subsequent UN publication on an 'Optional Protocol to the Convention on the Rights of the Child on the Sale of Children, Child Prostitution and Pornography' (2000) aimed to extend the protection of the rights of the child by advocating a 'holistic' approach which involved addressing socio-economic factors such as poverty and inequality as well as the trafficking of children (Lim 1998).

The work of ECPAT (End Child Prostitution for Sexual Purposes and Trafficking) has brought attention to child prostitution as a global phenomenon. ECPAT started its campaign in 1991 in Bangkok and aims to end child prostitution. After the First World Congress Against Commercial Sexual Exploitation of Children it has grown and now operates in over fifty countries (Spangenberg 2001). The emergence of organisations like ECPAT and the growing international concerns about children and young people involved in prostitution is a response in part to the growing commercialisation of the sex trade internationally involving an increasing number of those aged under

18 years of age, but it is also a function of changing conceptions of childhood. In most countries a distinction has emerged between childhood and adult prostitution and the former is becoming widely perceived as unacceptable. The changing public attitudes towards child prostitution is reflected in similar concerns about paedophilia and other forms of child sexual abuse (O'Connell Davidson 2005). Increasingly, young people are seen as 'innocent' and 'pure' and their involvement in prostitution as a form of 'slavery'. While the focus on protecting and removing those young people involved in prostitution has widespread international support, it has been suggested that the motives for limiting child prostitution may not be entirely philanthropic. As the scale of prostitution has increased in some countries to such an extent that it has become integrated into the economic, social and political life of these countries, the separation of child from adult prostitution has the effect of legitimising and rationalising the sex industry (Jeffreys 1999; 2000).

In the UK attention turned in the 1990s to the number of young people cautioned or convicted for prostitution-related offences. It was found between 1989 and 1993 that a total of 1,758 cautions were issued to young women under the age of eighteen in England and Wales. In the same period, 1,435 convictions were secured against young women under the age of 18 (Ayre and Barrett 2000; Lee and O'Brien 1995). The criminalisation of young people involved in prostitution came to be increasingly seen as either inappropriate or counterproductive. Such an approach, it was argued, failed to address the causes of their involvement while exonerating the adults who exploit and abuse the children. Organisations like the Children's Society and Barnardo's have argued that not only should children involved in prostitution be seen as victims of abuse but the clients who purchase their services should also be seen as child sex abusers and treated accordingly.

Although there is some uncertainty in England and Wales about the number of children involved in prostitution, research has found that even by the late 1990s that 48 agencies reported contact with 300 children under 16 years of age who were involved in clipping (taking money from a punter and then running away without exchanging sex) or were swapping sex for money, drugs, accommodation or other goods (van Meeuwen and Swann 1998). At the same time the focus shifted to the inadequacy of services for young people 'at risk' of engaging in prostitution.

In America it is estimated that there may be as many as 400,000 young people under 18 involved in prostitution, with approximately 5,000 in New York City alone (Spangenberg 2001). In Australia, 3,733 children were reported to be engaged in commercial sexual activities in 1997 with 300 young people participating in prostitution in Melbourne. An ECPAT survey in New Zealand found over 195 known cases of child prostitution, with 145 being under 16 years old (Saphira and Oliver 2002). In Canada, the Bagley report in 1984 transformed the professional discourse in relation to young people involved in prostitution, from seeing it as a form of juvenile delinquency to the sexual abuse of children. Juvenile prostitution was established as a new social priority and a range of protective and legislative measures were subsequently put in place to reduce the level of juvenile prostitution and prosecute adult clients (Brock 1998; Lowman 1987; 1992). The various studies that have been conducted in different countries demonstrate the growing preoccupation with young people and sexual exploitation, while at the same time generally identifying the limited range of services that are available to deal with this issue (Ennew et al. 1996).

Conclusion

Over the last two decades prostitution has moved up the social and political agenda. It is suggested that a number of factors have contributed to this change and influenced the way in which the issue of prostitution has been conceived and responded to. There have also been changes in the composition and organisation of prostitution, which has played a significant part in changing public sensibilities and perceptions. As we have seen, the issue of prostitution has mainly been seen as an issue of female street prostitution and the problem of prostitution has changed from one of public order to a medical issue and more recently a drugs-related issue. Subsequently, it has become increasingly associated with the changing patterns of migration and human trafficking.

There are also a number of other and less tangible influences that have affected the organisation of prostitution as well as public and political attitudes in recent years. These include the decline in the family, the growth of single parent households, growing use of more impersonal dating agencies, the proliferation of pornography, and most importantly, women's growing involvement in the labour market which has increased the possibility of legitimate employment for many women, albeit often in low paid, service occupations.

The changing structure of the labour market has no doubt had a number of more or less direct effects on the way in which prostitution is organised and assessed. On one level, the justification for engaging in prostitution because of a lack of legitimate job opportunities appears less tenable, while at the same time the increasing amount of relatively low paid service sector work for women has the effect of 'normalising' prostitution, which on face value at least begins to increasingly resemble conventional forms of employment. This development is particularly evident in the different forms of off-street prostitution.

Alongside these developments has been a significant growth in many countries of sex clubs in which the traditional distinctions between prostitution, striptease, lap dancing and hostessing are becoming increasingly blurred. At the same time the commercialisation of sexual services is increasingly becoming a part of 'ordinary work' and a feature of corporate entertainment (Bernstein 2001). It has also been noted that the post war transformation of San Francisco's tenderloin has involved the gradual suppression of street prostitution with a simultaneous expansion of new sites of commercial sex (Sides 2006).

Combined with the growth of different types of sex clubs is the expansion of the market in pornography, and there has been a growing use of the internet as a mechanism for accessing pornographic material, arranging dates as well as impersonal sexual contacts. Sites have also been established by 'punters' or 'johns' such as Punternet to provide information on the services available in different brothels, in order to share experiences and disseminate information. The growing commercialisation and impersonalisation of social and sexual encounters has no doubt provided an increased acceptance of the commercialisation of sexual relations that would appear to present prostitution as a more 'normal' activity. At the same time, we have seen what has been described as the 'commodification of pleasure' and the encouragement to 'consume' sex without commitment or effort. In today's consumer society there is a growing acceptance in some circles that it is legitimate to engage in more impersonal and short-term sexual relationships (Brewis and Linstead 2000). However, at the same time, the ready availability of sexual partners through the internet and in the growing number of clubs where people can go for spontaneous sexual encounters would seem to undermine the need to pay for such experiences.

Alongside this, there has been a growing preoccupation with eroticism divorced from both reproduction and love, which encourages the seeking of sexual delights for their own sake. As Zygmunt Bauman (1998) suggests this emerging 'no strings attached' postmodern eroticism, makes it increasingly possible 'to enter and leave any association of convenience, but is also easy prey to forces eager to exploit its seductive powers'. Bauman claims that we are becoming a world of sensation gatherers drawn towards what Anthony Giddens (1992) has referred to as 'plastic sex'. But while the postmodern world encourages the seeker to develop the full potential of the sexual subject, the same culture explicitly forbids treating another as a sexual object. As women increasingly come to take their place in the labour market and claim their rights as citizens and consumers, there is a consequent refusal to be treated as sex objects. The growing demand for 'plastic sex', on the one hand, and the increased emphasis on women's rights and equality on the other, has created a growing division. This growing divide, however, is being increasingly filled by foreign women who are seen not as 'our' wives and daughters, and who because of their immigrant status are currently unable to qualify as full citizens with accompanying rights.

A final factor, which has contributed to the changing response to prostitution, is the changing conceptions of public and private space. In a period in which many inner city areas have been regenerated and reconstituted the dynamics of space have changed profoundly. The changing use and meaning of space has conspired to affect attitudes towards street-based activities such as prostitution. Space is contested and the establishment of new moral landscapes reflect the unfolding relationships between the different dynamics of private relations on the one hand and 'lived' space of prostitution on the other (Hubbard and Sanders 2003).

These developments as we have seen, pull in different directions leading to a greater differentiation within prostitution, particularly between street and off street prostitution. They have also inspired a set of changing and uneven responses to the regulation of prostitution in different countries. On one side, we see the hardening of attitudes and the introduction of tougher and more punitive policies. At the other extreme, we see examples of greater liberalisation and tolerance. It is these variations and complexities which need further and detailed exploration, but before engaging in these issues directly, it is necessary to address some of the myths which have become associated with prostitution.

Chapter 2

Prostitution myths

Introduction

The whole subject of prostitution is shrouded in half-truths, false dichotomies and euphemisms. There are a number of recurring myths and misconceptions that permeate the literature which provide both an obstacle to theorising and act as an impediment to developing progressive and realistic policies.

The reasons for the continuing appeal of the myths surrounding prostitution are threefold. First, there has been a relatively limited amount of quality research carried out on prostitution during much of the post war period. Second, and relatedly, there has been a general lack of knowledge and interest in this issue, which has promoted a reliance on selective and limited accounts. Third, the mobilisation of myths can be a convenient way of avoiding counterfactual evidence of protecting one's preferred position. The reliance on the various myths outlined below is not limited to those who are new to this subject or to inexperienced researchers or writers. Rather, they are endemic in the literature and the road to policy formation is cluttered by the conceptual obstacles that they generate.

The term 'myth' is not used here to suggest that the propositions discussed below are entirely false. Indeed, if they were simply wrong it would be difficult to explain their widespread adoption. Most myths have a rational core, although in some cases this core is extremely thin and weak. In line with Roland Barthes (1973) the term 'myth' is used to suggest that these propositions constitute at best a partial or one-sided account and that in some cases they may involve exaggerations or distortions. As Barthes argues the proliferation of myths removes contradictions and reduces the richness of reality. Moreover, by substituting half-truths, platitudes and slogans for explanations, myths all too easily distort and cheapen analysis. Such accounts individually or cumulatively skew collective understanding such that developing informed, rational and realistic policies becomes extremely difficult.

One of the aims of 'unmasking' these mythological accounts is to try to develop a more consistent and comprehensive account of these phenomena.

In doing so I will draw on a range of empirical material, although recognising that the research on this issue has often been conducted by researchers who explicitly or implicitly adhere to some or all of these myths and the research itself is conceptualised within a limited or distorted conceptual framework. Thus identifying the limitations of some of the more popular myths, which surround prostitution, is at the same time a path-clearing exercise. It is, however, a necessary first step toward understanding and appreciating the potential viability of available policy options.

In this chapter the aim is to critically review some of the prevalent myths, albeit in a necessarily brief and at times cursory way. A full examination of these myths would necessarily have to examine the assumptions and meta-theories on which they are based. Instead, the aim here is to engage in a reconsideration of these often taken-for-granted conceptions and to develop an awareness of how these (mis)conceptions shape views on prostitution and in turn affect policy formation.

As will become evident these myths are often interconnected and mutually reinforcing. It is also the case that some of the more popular and widely used myths are the most untenable. The notion for example that prostitution is 'the oldest profession' although having little in the way of any historical justification is quoted ad nauseam. This widely adopted proposition has, however, proved to be one of the greatest impediments to the development of reforms in relation to prostitution and it is therefore necessary to deal with it first.

The oldest profession

The frequently made claim that prostitution is 'the oldest profession', is often used to suggest the inherent limits to any form of intervention aimed at radically changing or improving the current situation. It is at heart a defeatist statement that has connotations of both fatalism and naturalism. Commentators, who tend to have limited understanding of history or prostitution, often churn out this line because they believe it makes them look knowledgeable. In reality, it displays a remarkable ignorance. Strategically, the sub-text of this statement is that the author is not really interested in serious discussion about social reform. We should therefore always be wary of people who make such claims in policy arenas.

The establishment of professions such as banking, medicine and law in the eighteenth and nineteenth centuries was designed to protect standards and the remuneration of their members, while at the same time promote their collective interests. In relation to these objectives prostitution has never come close to achieving the status of a profession. On the contrary, as an activity it has historically been conspicuously fragmented, individualistic and non-professionalised. It has been widely associated with social and geographical exclusion, stigmatisation and moral indignation.

Even amongst those who agree that to talk of prostitution as a profession is a misnomer it is still often claimed that there is some historic continuity between the provision of sexual services for 'payment and reward' which dates back to 'primitive' societies and is manifest in so-called 'temple prostitution' (Scott 1996). However, as Engels (1972) noted, the provision of sexual services to strangers and visitors which was reported in some early patriarchal societies had little or nothing to do with prostitution, as we understand it, but was rather seen as a service provided to visitors and strangers by single women in the village. The notion of hetaerism, which is often taken as synonymous with Greek prostitution, is according to Engels 'directly traceable to group marriage, to the sacrificial surrender of the woman whereby they purchased their right to chastity' (1972: 75). It was only with the development of monogamy, Engels claims, that prostitution in its modern form began to emerge. Similarly, Michel Foucault (1985) in his account of *The Use of Pleasure* notes that the Greeks distinguished between those who had many relationships (hetairekos) and those that prostituted themselves by taking payment for their services (pepornuemenon). Significantly, young men who prostituted themselves in passive mode were barred from office and were derided for 'feminising' themselves. At a later date the draconian sanctions against any form of sodomy together with the growing antipathy to male prostitution made prostitution, formally at least, overwhelmingly heterosexual with women 'servicing' men. Thus the institutionalisation of prostitution from medieval times has overwhelmingly involved women acting as prostitutes (Karras 1996).

Although there were a series of ordinances, which closed down brothels in the medieval period, and prostitutes were banned from certain urban centres from time to time – amid long periods of toleration – it was not until the nineteenth century, according to Judith Walkowitz (1977), that street prostitutes emerged as an identifiable outcast group. Before this period she argues prostitution was not generally viewed as a specialised occupation and arguably it is only at this point that it becomes possible to talk about prostitution as a career. Even the development of a widespread and elaborate system of enforced and voluntary registration of prostitutes across Europe in the nineteenth century, in itself, did not transform prostitution into a 'profession'. And although Parent-Duchalet (1836) referred to 'public prostitutes' as constituting a 'class apart', Alain Corbin (1990) in his incisive account of prostitution in France argues that even the registration of prostitutes following the passing of the Contagious Diseases Acts 'indicated the adoption not of a profession, for prostitution could not be regarded as such, but of the state of being'.

Although the stereotype of the career prostitute remains prevalent in popular representations it remains the case that many women involved in prostitution are short term and sporadic participants. Indeed research indicates that the majority of women involved in prostitution aim to do it for a limited period of time, although in some cases women find it difficult to leave and stay involved in prostitution for longer than intended (Matthews 1986a: Sanders 2005).

The problem with certain 'histories' is they take the present day situation as their starting point and look back in history and anything that remotely resembles current practices is automatically seen as being a precursor to the present. In this form of evolutionism the present is projected backwards and history is seen as the gradual unfolding of the present. Since many accounts of prostitution take this evolutionary or historicist form the 'history' of prostitution is still to be written.

There are variations in the 'the oldest profession' theme, which are equally suspect. These include statements like; 'It has always been with us', or alternatively: 'Where there is a demand, the supply will follow.' The employment of these mythological statements serves to evaporate history and places the burden of explanation on the 'irresponsibility of man' or it is seen as a function of 'human nature' or in some cases as a product of trans-historical male sexual needs.

One of the current variants of the 'oldest profession' myth is the claim that we should adopt a 'pragmatic' approach and accept the existence of prostitution and that rather than trying to change or reduce it we should simply try to manage it in the most cost effective way (Cusick, Martin and May 2003). However, the fact that activities such as violence, theft, drug use and the like are likely to be with us in the future does not mean that their form, meaning and impact has not changed significantly over time. Nor does it mean that either we accept them as they are, or refrain from trying to develop interventions to reduce their prevalence and effects.

Prostitution as a response to male sexual needs

One of the enduring justifications for the continuing existence of both female and heterosexual and male homosexual prostitution is that it is a natural or inevitable response to male sexual needs. If men are unmarried, away from home, shy or disabled there is a need, it is argued, for sexual services to be supplied by a prostitute. For all those men with exotic and unusual tastes that are not fully satisfied in marriage, an accessible 'outlet' or 'release' is required (Weatherall and Priestly 2001). Employing a hydraulic model of sexuality in which men are seen to 'demand' sex and women to 'supply' it means there is very little discussion of women's sexual needs or desires. As Mary McIntosh puts it;

> We often take these everyday beliefs and experiences as evidence of the eternal nature of differences between the sexes. Sex, after all, is something we think of as very 'natural' – you do it with little or no equipment and with no clothes on. But nothing could be further from the truth. There

may be a generic 'sex' drive which is natural, but specific ways in which it will be expressed, and indeed whether these will be recognizably 'sexual' at all, depends on the way in which the individual handles the general culture and the specific life experiences she confronts.

(McIntosh 1978: 55)

The claim that the sexual drive is like other natural needs such as 'hunger' is a misplaced analogy. There are various ways of satisfying male sexual urges without recourse to others, let alone prostitutes. As Carole Pateman (1991) has argued, unlike needs such as food or shelter no one has ever died for want of an outlet for their sexual needs.

As sexologists have demonstrated, sex is a highly scripted and culturally conditioned activity (Plummer 1975; Weeks 2003). Far from being 'natural' it is a complex and socially constructed phenomenon. Contemporary patterns of sexuality in advanced western societies are far from universal or natural. The expression of sexuality cannot be read off from biological givens. Sexual scripts are to some extent learned responses, which are acquired through socialisation processes and are shaped by cultural norms. as well as by economic and structural differentials. What is significant in relation to prostitution is how men come to define the experience of having a sexual relation with a female prostitute as potentially pleasurable and how they come to believe that their sexual desires can be met through this type of paid-for impersonal association. In the literature, some clients say that they are looking for companionship and some form of personal contact and even a relationship. The female prostitute on the other hand is looking at the clock and thinking about the money. In the majority of cases she performs a well-rehearsed act which covers up her indifference or contempt.

The research on clients, whilst relatively limited, indicates that rather than being lonely, single, physically deformed, shy or individuals with extreme sexual preferences, they are drawn from a cross section of the male population and that many are married or have regular partners (Coy et al. 2007; McLeod 1982: Matthews 1986a). In fact, research carried out by Brooks-Gordon and Gelsthorpe (2003) which recorded the initial statements made by kerb crawlers at the point of arrest, found that one of the most common statements that was made by those who attempted to deny that they were seeking out the services of a prostitute was: 'But officer I am a married man.' One police officer was quoted in the same research report as saying: 'Most kerb-crawlers are married, they're just looking for something a bit different to what they get at home.' Rather than being motivated by a desperate sexual need, most of the kerb-crawlers interviewed said that they were visiting the area because they were 'curious'; or 'just looking' or were seeking 'entertainment'. Other studies that have examined the motivation of clients have found that men who pay for sex have a number of other sexual partners (Ward et al. 2005), while others report that they use prostitutes either because they want a variety of partners or sexual practices, or because of the ease of the transaction (Bailey 2002; McKegney and Barnard 1996; Monto 2000; Pitts et al. 2004). Research conducted in Canada based on a sample of 365 'johns' found that:

> The average age at which they first purchased sex was 24 years. When we asked them what prompted their first visit to a sex seller, 5% said pornography, 12% said 'friends', 27% reported that it had been a spontaneous decision and 41% said that it was the availability and/or visibility of sex workers.
>
> (Lowman and Atchinson 2006: 288)

The significant proportion of men who either made a spontaneous decision or were motivated by the visibility and availability of 'sex workers' suggests that the purchase of sexual services is much more opportunistic than is generally assumed. At the same time the relation between the male buyer and the female seller cannot be reduced to an exchange of sexual services. As a number of feminists have pointed out the relationship is invariably underpinned by differential power relations (O'Connell-Davidson 1998; O'Neill 2001).

In a similar vein, some feminists have argued that the use and abuse of the female prostitute's body is an expression of male violence (Barry 1995). Thus, it is argued that rather than prostitution being a natural expression of male sexual needs its functioning serves to reinforce and reify the patriarchal ideology of male dominance (Kesler 2002; Scoular 2004). Prostitution is also seen to support the 'double standard' of sexual norms by which women are castigated for being promiscuous while male promiscuity is seen as a sign of potency (Jeffreys 1997). The claim that the existence of prostitution serves to reduce rape and sexual assaults is also rejected by most feminists who argue that the visibility and institutionalisation of prostitution itself serves to present women as legitimate objects of sexual violence. The myth of male sexual needs is often presented in relation to the claim that prostitution is the oldest profession. In this way these two propositions become mutually reinforcing, since both tend to construct prostitution as inevitable and the issue is framed in terms of the most appropriate way of meeting this 'demand' (Raymond 2004).

A non-victim crime

It is often suggested that prostitution is a non-victim crime. Edwin Schur (1965) defined a non-victim crime as 'the willing exchange, among adults, of a strongly demanded but legally proscribed goods and services' and that 'crimes without victims may be limited to those situations in which one person obtains from another, in a fairly direct exchange, a commodity or personal service which is socially disapproved of and legally proscribed'. He does not discuss the issue of prostitution specifically, but in subsequent discussions of 'crimes without victims' prostitution is seen as an issue that should be included (Meier and Geis 1997).

One of the main characteristics of victimless crimes, Schur argues, is that they lack direct complainants and consequently problems arise in producing and presenting evidence. The private nature of such transactions also serves to make enforcement problematic. Consequently, it leaves the door open for corruption and misuse of the law. Indeed, it is suggested that the operation of the law can be detrimental to the self-image of the individual and the consequent stigmatisation may propel them into criminality; or alternatively stimulate the creation of criminal subcultures and the expansion of illicit markets. At the same time, it is suggested, legal controls can inadvertently increase the demand for these illicit services.

In Schur's three case studies of non-victim crimes – abortion, homosexuality and drug use – it is clear that there are very different interpersonal, moral, and social dynamics in play. Public attitudes towards each of these activities vary greatly and the individual and social impact can be very different. At the same time anti-abortionists, for example, do not believe that there is not a victim; while the families and communities which are affected by the prevalence of certain types of drug use undoubtedly see themselves, as well as their relatives and acquaintances, as victims to some degree.

Prostitution raises issues, which are very different from those raised by abortion, homosexuality and drug use and involves different forms of victimisation. To argue that prostitution is a non-victim crime is to adopt a very narrow and superficial definition of victimisation. Indeed, it might be suggested that what characterises prostitution is the extremely diverse forms of victimisation which are often associated with it. Indeed, it is almost certainly the case that those involved in prostitution, particularly street prostitution, are one of the most highly victimised social groups. The victims associated with prostitution include not only the women themselves but also their children, families and dependents as well as residents who live in red light districts.

Amongst the most obvious victims are the women themselves who in many cases have long histories of abuse, neglect and exclusion. Research on the aetiology of female prostitutes has consistently identified the following factors as being associated with entry into prostitution – physical sexual abuse, parental neglect, being in local authority care and drug addiction. Moreover, these experiences are compounded by their relatively high incidence of homelessness, unemployment and poverty. The increased vulnerability and low self esteem which many of these young women experience makes them easy targets for pimps and others who want to exploit them and groom them for prostitution. These forms of victimisation, abuse and neglect have until recently received a generally muted response in official circles, because those involved are seen as 'damaged goods' and drawn from marginalised and 'outcast' populations. They are always somebody else's daughters and somebody else's wife or partner.

In general, it is very difficult to find women involved in prostitution – particularly those on the street – who do not experience consistent levels of victimisation. Indeed, in many cases they are subject to multiple victimisation and this victimisation is compounded over a period of time. While some have argued that entry into prostitution is for some women at least a way of taking control of their lives and reducing their vulnerability the reality is in many cases that their involvement in prostitution heightens and extends the range of victimisation which they experience.

Apart from the women themselves, the involvement in prostitution can have adverse effects upon their children and their social and interpersonal relations. Children can be put at risk, suffer from neglect, be placed in care, and in general be subject to cycles of disadvantage. While there are no doubt some prostitutes who are exemplary mothers and work hard to send their children to good schools, these cases are the exception rather than the rule.

Other victims include residents, particularly women who live in red-light districts who suffer from noise, litter, abuse and general problems of disorder. Red light districts normally arise in the more deprived inner-city areas, which often have more than their fair share of social problems. The presence of prostitution can have an extremely detrimental effect on the quality of life in these areas. It is also the case that for many women living in deprived inner city areas that an informal curfew operates which makes them reticent to go out unaccompanied in the evening. In red light areas these fears tend to be exacerbated (Hubbard 1998). It has also been argued by radical feminists that it is women in general who are indirect victims of prostitution, as a result of the objectification of women, which is perpetuated through heterosexual prostitution.

Given the range of victimisation which is associated with prostitution there is an ongoing debate as to whether prostitution involving consenting adults should be the law's business. This debate was most clearly articulated in an exchange between Lord Devlin (1965) and H. L. Hart (1962), with the former outlining the conservative approach and the latter presenting the liberal position. Hart maintains that prostitution is a 'non-victim' crime' and a 'private' and individual matter and therefore 'not the law's business'. Lord Devlin, in contrast, maintains that 'morality' is by definition a social rather than an individual matter. He maintains that the law is based upon this social morality and that therefore society has a duty to enforce moral norms and safeguard communities through the law. Devlin also argues that the stigmatisation associated with prostitution is not a function of the law but rather is embedded in public attitudes and social norms. The crux of the debate, as Tim Newburn (1992) has pointed out, is that while liberals like Hart claim that the role of the law is to 'protect one man from another' the conservative position is that one of the main roles of the law is to punish 'moral wicked-ness' or as Devlin puts it 'to enforce a moral principal'. Since Devlin claims that allowing sexual immorality threatens the existence of society. Hart, in reply, accuses him of moving from 'the acceptable position that *some* shared morality is essential to the existence of any society, to the unacceptable position that society is identical with its morality'.

The polemic, however, gravitates towards extremes and while many liberals would like to see a reduction in the level of legal control of prostitution most would also want to see laws designed to protect individuals from exploitation and corruption and would support the rights of residents and other social groups to be protected from noise, nuisance and intimidation. At the same time, while most would agree that the law is always to some degree an expres-sion of public attitudes and norms and that communities ought to be pro-tected, that the conservative vision of 'community' is too heterogeneous and does not allow for the diversity of modern social relations (Young 1990). The enduring danger, however, of the claim that 'prostitution is not the law's business' is that it can create a sense of ambivalence and uncertainty about the need to intervene in relation to exploitation, commercialisation, overt or covert forms of coercion, as well as in relation to problems of disorder.

Women enter prostitution out of 'free choice'

There is a deep division in the literature between liberals on one hand who claim that women's involvement in prostitution is a matter of 'free choice' and radical feminists on the other who argue that the notion of 'choice' in this context is a misnomer and that women are 'forced' into prostitution as a result of either poverty, deprivation, unequal gender and power relations or simply as a result of coercion (Doezema 2002; Jeffreys 1997: Barry 1995; O'Connell-Davidson 1998).

Those who claim that women's involvement in prostitution is a matter of 'free choice' tend to see the prostitute as a rational actor operating in an open and roughly equal market society. Liberals depict the women concerned as self-directed decision-makers who are attracted to prostitution because either it fits with their lifestyle, the promise of earning large amounts of money, or because they enjoy engaging in 'erotic labour' (Chapkis 1997).

This debate is in turn a function of the yet unresolved agency/structure debate that plagues the social sciences (Giddens 1979). Some feminists have taken exception to the depiction of women as passive victims and have been critical of structuralist accounts which they claim deny women agency (McNay 2000). However, in emphasising agency against structure and forcibly arguing that those involved in prostitution are not just the passive victims of circum-stances there is a tendency to use the terms 'choice' and particularly 'free choice' in a way that misrepresents the actual processes of decision-making involved in entering prostitution. The outcome is to present the process in terms which are too voluntaristic and individualistic and which implicitly or explicitly involve a lack of appreciation of the social and structural processes in play.

The decision to enter any form of work in contemporary society is subject to different levels of constraint. These constraints operate at the economic, social and personal levels. On the economic level within the capitalist labour market all workers are 'free' to sell their labour as they wish. However, this 'free' labour is compelled to sell its labour power or starve. Thus underpinning this freedom is a form of compulsion. Those engaging in prostitution formally have the same choice as other sectors of the workforce and in principal enjoy the same level of unfreedom. However, the labour market is highly segmented and access to different forms of employment is a function of education and skills while the labour market is differentiated along the lines of class, age, gender and location. We know that many of those entering prostitution have low educational levels and few skills and therefore their choice in the market is generally restricted to the poorly paid, temporary and menial jobs.

Alongside these restrictions of choice the available research indicates that many of those entering prostitution have a marginalised and stigmatised status before entering prostitution and a significant proportion have criminal records, have spent time in institutions and are heavy drug users (Cusick, Martin and May 2003; Hester and Westmarland 2004). All of these elements restrict the choice of occupation even further and particularly those who are heavy drug users find it difficult to secure paid employment either because the employers will not hire them or because they find it difficult to keep to normal work routines. Moreover, the types of menial jobs that might be available would probably not pay enough to sustain their drug habit. Thus for many who are heavy drug users there is no real choice between working in a low paid job or engaging in prostitution since it is only the latter which can provide the level of earnings required. We also know that a significant percentage of heavy drug users involved in prostitution work to support the drug habit of their partners/pimps. In this scenario the notion of 'choice' and certainly 'free choice' has little relevance to the situation in which those engaging in prostitution find themselves.

On the social level the buying and selling of sexual services is highly gendered. The decision to sell sexual services is not so much governed by a woman's decision to 'choose' prostitution or not, but is structured by relations of domination and subordination and a corresponding ideology which signals that men have the right to demand that women's bodies are sold on the market. Domination operates not so much as overt coercion or force, but is embedded within a range of institutions that tacitly presuppose the legitimacy of this relation. Even when women express agency, this agency may appear to take the form of self-actualisation, but tends to be appropriated by the clients, pimps and entrepreneurs. It is not a form of agency that is centred around the expression of the sexual interests of the women involved in prostitution but involves what Kathy Miriam (2005) describes as 'disembodied agency'. Miriam argues that the inability of the liberal 'sex work' theorists to grasp the ways in which agency is structured and gendered leads to a reduction of the power relations involved to an opposition of coercion on one side and freedom on the other:

> The pro-sex-work theory assumes that victimization and agency are mutually exclusive and points to prostitutes' ability to negotiate over aspects of their work conditions as evidence that prostitutes have agency. The expressivist version of this theory interprets prostitutes practice of negotiation as in and of itself constituting a *creative reworking* of the existing sexual order. But from this same theoretical vantage point, one aspect of the sexual order remains *non*negotiable and thus unworkable, namely men's right to be sexually serviced. There is a blind spot in this pro-sex-work theory where this 'right' remains invisible as such, partly because male power is invisible to it as *domination* and only intelligible as coercive force. Thus blinkered, the theory constructs sex workers as 'free' unless forcibly coerced into prostitution: the theory argues that if prostitutes have this 'freedom', they cannot therefore be said to be 'victims'.
>
> (Miriam 2005: 13–14)

If these economic and social processes in combination act to restrict the available options to a point where choice is extremely limited, the personal histories of many of those involved in prostitution is characterised by years of physical and sexual abuse and neglect. These experiences have consequences for an individual's self esteem and sense of self-worth. For those who have histories of sexual abuse, engaging in prostitution may be seen as a less traumatic event, while psychologists suggest that many of those who are abused as children are prone to other forms of abuse later in life. In addition overt coercion plays a significant role in the decision to engage in prostitution. Coercion from pimps is reported to be the primary reason for entry for some 10–15 per cent of women working on the street; while overt coercion is reported to account for approximately 15 per cent of those who are victims of trafficking and end up in off-street locations in the UK (Kelly and Regan 2003; O'Neill 1997).

A considerable proportion of those who are involved in prostitution combine economic disadvantage with forms of marginalisation, stigmatisation and exclusion as well as histories of abuse and neglect. Cumulatively, these processes serve to restrict choice and channel these women into prostitution. Thus, engaging in prostitution cannot be seen as an expression of 'free choice'. Rather, prostitution is something that people turn to when they run out of choices.

To a large extent, however, the discussion of choice in relation to the labour market is irrelevant since the majority of those who become involved in prostitution do so as children. That is, the research on age of entry into prostitution repeatedly shows that the majority first become involved under the age of eighteen. These young women are not making rational choices about different forms of employment but are rather becoming caught up in prostitution at an early age. For this reason some commentators prefer to identify the process of entry into prostitution not so much as one of a conscious weighing up of the options but rather as a less deliberate process of 'drift' (Matza 1964).

The debate regarding choice has been reconstructed in relation to trafficking, and those who migrate to other countries to sell sexual services have been divided into those who do so voluntarily and those who are forced. This dichotomy however, which has now found its way into the official European lexicon does not do justice to the complexity of the decision-making process involved. In most of the discussions on this topic the voluntary/coerced distinction is only mobilised at the point at which movement across borders takes place. The coercion, pressure and constraints which provide the backdrop against which the decision to sell sexual services in a foreign country are rarely referred to, while coercion is normally defined narrowly as physical coercion. Instead of developing a form of analysis which is able to transcend or move beyond the coercion/consent opposition some liberal critics simply aim to minimise the role which different forms of coercion play and tend to present the women involved as willing victims (Doezema 1998).

There is a further tension that runs through the liberal model. Since involvement in prostitution is seen as the exercise of 'free choice' by a rational actors this has implications for notions of responsibility and culpability. Since these rational actors are held to be fully aware that they are engaging in an occupation which involves illegalities, social stigmatisation and marginalisation there can be little or no defence against the sanctions that they receive as a result of engaging in these activities. At the same time there is little justification for welfare provision or social support. Moreover, there seems little point in developing 'exiting' programmes and the like since just as these women have exercised 'free choice' when entering prostitution so they can be expected to exercise the same 'free choice' in making decisions on whether or not to continue in prostitution.

The fact that there are now a growing number of support agencies and programmes in the UK designed to help women leave prostitution suggests that there is a recognition that women do not enter prostitution out of 'free choice' and that once involved in prostitution their ability to make personally beneficial decisions often decreases. As some radical feminists have argued, underpinning the notion of 'free choice' is the sense that it is women who are responsible for creating and maintaining prostitution. Since engaging in prostitution is an expression of voluntarism by the women concerned the role of men, or more precisely clients, is concealed and inadvertently justified in relation to the choice made by individual women. Jeffreys (1997), for example, argues that prostitution is not about choice for women but choice for men.

From a similar vantage point Kathleen Barry (1995), who sees prostitution as form of 'sexual slavery', points out that slavery cannot be understood in relation to the notion of 'consent'. A slave may consent to perform certain services for her master but giving this 'consent' does not affect the structural relations involved or the level of oppression. While there are clearly elements of slavery involved in prostitution it is an exaggeration to see all forms of prostitution as slavery. However, the point that choices are made within asymmetrical relations of power and that the exercise of choice does not necessarily change those relations is valid.

One way in which the advocates of 'free choice' attempt to support their position is by providing quotations from those involved in prostitution who claim that engaging in prostitution was a positive decision. Prostitutes, like people working in other occupations are always prone to put a positive gloss on what they do, particularly if they feel that that is what the researcher wants to hear. It is not that in their day to day life that those involved in prostitution, particularly street prostitutes, do exercise some choice about where and when they work, the selection of clients, how much to charge and what services they are prepared to provide. In terms of the intimacy of the encounter with the client they may also exercise some degree of 'control' over the interaction and exercise certain limited degrees of power. But in the final analysis the power relation is asymmetrical with the balance of power leaning heavily towards the purchaser rather than the provider.

In sum, the liberal model that sees involvement in prostitution as the product of individual choice tends to lose sight of the structural and social factors that nurture and encourage this trade in sexual services and which shape the market. These structures and the dynamics that sustain them are not reducible to individual choice. To begin to understand how choice is structured by gender, class and age it is worth reminding ourselves that adult men tend not purchase sexual services so much from adult men but rather from 'rent boys', women do not routinely buy sexual services from other adult women, poor people do not buy sexual services from rich people and young people do not as a rule pay for the sexual services of older people.

It's just a job like any other

Closely related to the liberal notion that involvement in prostitution is a matter of 'free choice' is the contention that prostitution is just a job like any other. In an attempt to normalise prostitution some commentators argue that whatever its advantages or disadvantages may be, prostitution should be seen as a legitimate form of work (Doezema 1998). Indeed, in recent years there has been a growing support in some countries for normalising prostitution as a legitimate form of work. The International Labour Organization (ILO) has called for prostitution to be recognised as a legitimate economic activity and suggest that this would be particularly beneficial to poorer countries since it could be an important source of revenue through taxation (Lim 1998).

The normalisation of prostitution can be seen as a response to the claims of the radicals and conservatives that it is a demeaning and soul-destroying activity. In contrast, liberals argue that prostitution is no more demeaning than working in sweatshops or engaging in other menial service occupations. Moreover, the reportedly high levels of remuneration associated with prostitution, it is suggested, helps to mitigate the pains and stresses commonly associated with 'sex work' (Brewis and Linstead 2000). It is also suggested that, like all service occupations, prostitution involves the sale of a range of skills and services on the market and that, morality aside, providing sexual services is really no different from selling one's intellect, skills or other attributes. The sale of sexual services, it is argued, is just another type of contractual relationship.

But despite the claims that a prostitute is merely selling her labour power, it is the case as Carole Pateman (1988) has argued that the services provided by prostitutes, unlike other forms of service provision, cannot be separated from the person and most importantly from the person's consciousness. It is the intimacy of the sexual exchange that constructs prostitution as a unique service. That is, the prostitute's identity often becomes inseparable from the activity. Consequently, the sale of sexual services is inextricably related to a person's sense of self.

The issue of whether it is possible for a person to disassociate the selling of sexual services from their sense of self forms one of the main points of contention between liberal and radical feminists. Liberals, on one side, claim that women can have intimate sexual relations with a large variety of customers without feeling devalued or defiled, while the radical feminists argue that it is extremely difficult to disassociate these very intimate exchanges from other aspects of one's life (O'Connell Davidson 2002).

Reports by prostitutes themselves are replete with examples of how they try to distance themselves from their work. Many report that they experience revulsion and regret in relation to their occupation and that they increasingly find clients and in some cases men in general repulsive as well as often experiencing shame and guilt (Hoigard and Finstad 1992). They also develop rationalisations and techniques of neutralisation in order to try maintain a sense of self. If women are to remain in prostitution then it is necessary for the women concerned to develop rationalisations and strategies in order to keep their identities intact (Phoenix 2000; McKeganey and Barnard 1996). There is a qualitative distinction between women who have sex for money once or twice or those who occasionally use sex as a vehicle for acquiring gifts, promotion or other benefits and those who come to see themselves as nothing more than a prostitute. One such person, Lois aged 21, expresses this difference well:

> It hit me when I was 19 that I was actually a prostitute. I didn't really think about it before – it was just work. But then it hit me. I was actually selling myself. I was just a hole. I was nothing more than a body men paid to fuck. I was a prostitute.
>
> (quoted in Phoenix 2000: 44)

Carole Pateman (1988) has argued convincingly in opposition to the contractualists that prostitution is bound up with notions of masculinity and feminity. Unlike other service occupations in which bodily functions or services are traded, when a man enters into a prostitution contract he is not interested in a disembodied or impersonal service but rather he contracts to buy the use of a woman for a given period. Emphasising that prostitution involves a social as well as an individual relation Pateman argues that the man is buying not just a specific service but mastery of the woman's body. She argues that:

> Of course, men can also confirm their masculinity in other ways, but, in relations between the sexes, unequivocal affirmation is obtained by engaging in 'the sex act'. Womanhood, too, is confirmed in sexual activity, and when a prostitute contracts the use of her body she is thus selling *herself* in a very real sense. Women's selves are involved in prostitution in a different manner from the involvement of the self in other occupations. Workers of all kinds may be more or less 'bound up with their work', but the integral connection between sexuality and sense of the self means that, for self-protection, a prostitute must distance herself from her sexual use.
>
> (Pateman 1988: 207)

Those who argue that there is no real difference between prostitution and other forms of intimate contact linked to work such as 'straight' massage fail to recognise the profound significance that impersonal forms of sexual activity involving vaginal or anal penetration have in contemporary society. The punitive response to rape in most countries and the refusal to treat rape as just another form of interpersonal violence highlights the enormous significance that impersonal and unwanted forms of sexual penetration have in our lives. Significantly, prostitutes that have had sex with clients, who have then refused to pay, have brought charges of rape against them: while clients who have sex with underage girls – whether they pay or not – are in fact in most countries committing statutory rape. Indicatively, one 'call girl' has described engaging in prostitution as 'consenting to be raped for money' (Saner 2007).

The happy hooker

Despite the extensive research material, which has documented over the years in great detail the problems, and pressures, which many of those involved in prostitution face on a daily basis, there persists the image, or rather the fantasy, of the 'happy hooker'. This depiction of the prostitute is promoted in the media and endorsed by those who want to believe that involvement in prostitution is a matter of 'free choice'. Popular films such as *Klute*, and *Pretty Woman* present an image of the prostitute as independent, self-motivated and confident women who apparently remain untouched and untarnished by their involvement in prostitution. *Pretty Woman* in particular is an interesting film since it provides a feminised version of the American Dream by which women who use their involvement in commercialised sex are able to go from 'rags to riches'. The reality for most prostitutes is, however, the reverse. Behind the façade of independence and autonomy there are a large number of disillusioned women, whose sense of self-worth is continually being eroded. This process becomes more acute as women get older and their looks fade and their marketability declines. As Nanette Davis explains:

> The 'happy hooker' myth is a compilation of beliefs and usually errone-ous assumptions that portray a streetwise, sexy 'pretty woman' who freely chooses to enter prostitution. She enjoys her job, until 'the right man comes along', and in the meantime, finds sexual gratification from prostitution. A subtext suggests that a few fortunate, and extremely beautiful, women become wealthy in prostitution, or acquire riches by seducing a wealthy man. Prostitution is also depicted as 'empowering' women. By reversing the standard gender roles, the prostitute has the edge over the mere 'trick', and prostitution offers an avenue for sexual liberation. Empowerment is inevitable when women choose the 'life' over a forty-hour-a-week dull job, for prostitutes are free agents who can work preferred hours in the absence of a time clock and a boss. The 'happy hooker' myth suggests that prostitution is lucrative, glamorous and sexy.
>
> (Davis 2000: 139–40)

Associated with this conception of the 'happy hooker' is an underlying belief that women enjoy selling sex and that this gives them a real sense of independence (Dalla 2000). Closely attached to the notion of the 'happy hooker' is the concept of the prostitute having a 'heart of gold'. In these depictions the emphasis is either on the 'high life' and the potential earnings, or alternatively that prostitutes are a caring group of people who are providing sexual and emotional support to lonely, single men. There is in these accounts a conspicuous silence concerning the number of women involved in prostitution who are damaged, distressed or depressed. It is also the case that despite the potential earnings which are available from prostitution that the majority of women who have been interviewed tend to live in relative poverty.

Taking on the identity of a prostitute has a number of consequences – mostly negative – about how people come to see themselves and how they come to be viewed by others. These range from stigmatisation to social rejection and isolation, which produces a self-confirming dynamic of social exclusion. At the same time these conceptions are often accompanied by feelings of guilt and remorse. These negative feelings, which are widely reported in the literature, may stimulate the use of alcohol and mind numbing drugs in order for prostitutes to distance themselves from these problems. However, this in turn can create further problems of dependence and desperation.

The cycle of depression and exclusion, although common, is not inevitable. Different individuals are remarkably adept at dealing with this situation and the resilience of some women in the face of these experiences, as a number of commentators have noted, can be remarkable (see Phoenix 1999). However, such women are more properly seen as 'survivors' in what is a very demanding and grueling occupation. Happiness, on the other hand is not an emotion which is in reality often associated with prostitution and whatever independence and financial gains may accrue from prostitution it is based on a thousand dependencies.

Not surprisingly, most women involved in prostitution, according to the available research, do not stay in the business long (Matthews 1986a; Sanders 2005). Even those who were more committed and prepared to travel to find a suitable place to work tend to remain in prostitution for around three to five years. In many cases this was much longer than they had planned for. For some women their involvement in prostitution is a response to crisis in their lives – financial or otherwise – or the consequence of inducements, pressure or coercion. For them, prostitution is not an activity to be enjoyed but rather a response, however painful and distasteful, to their current predicament. Thus, engaging in prostitution is not for the vast majority of women a route to finding a wealthy partner, but is more likely to create contempt and mistrust of men, particularly clients.

Prostitution as (white) slavery

Just as some liberal feminists want to claim that prostitution is a job like any other and that women enter prostitution out of 'free choice' so radical feminists at the other extreme claim that prostitution is a form of sexual slavery and that is an expression of violence against women. Kathleen Barry (1979), for example, argues that sexual slavery comes in two main forms – one interpersonal involving fathers and brothers and pimps, who use and abuse women and girls – the other takes an institutional form involving brothels and harems. These organised forms are highly profitable. Thus for Barry:

Female sexual slavery is present in all situations where women or girls cannot change their immediate conditions of their existence; where regardless of how they got into those conditions, they cannot get out; and where they are subject to sexual violence and exploitation.

(Barry 1979: 283)

Female sexual slavery is, according to Barry, pervasive throughout patriarchal society. Prostitution is one of the more visible and insidious forms of sexual slavery. In a situation of sexual slavery all intercourse according to Barry is, by definition, rape.

Some writers have defined 'slavery' as those situations in which individuals' ability to negotiate is controlled by another person, or where another person has the power to decide how many clients or what 'services' are to be performed (Bindman 1997). Within this definition many of those women who work in brothels may be considered to be working in conditions of slavery. Thus there can be little doubt that prostitution in its different forms in different parts of the world involves significant elements of slavery. In its most dramatic form it involves women who have been abducted and coerced and forced to have sex with a number of clients against their will. The recent case of Natascha Kampusch who was abducted at the age of ten in Vienna and then imprisoned in an underground cellar brought international attention to this issue. In this home-made dungeon she was subjected to eight years of sexual abuse and was, significantly, required to call her captor 'master' (Harding 2006).

A number of similar but less well-publicised cases have been documented by Victor Malarek (2004) who provides a moving and compelling account of how young Russian girls – so-called 'Natashas' – have been duped, abducted, and sold by entrepreneurs with transactions often facilitated by trusted professionals, including police officers. He describes a situation in which 18 year old Russian girls who were leaving an orphanage were offered a job training as Chinese cooks which involved travelling to China:

About 30 girls signed up – all, not surprisingly pretty, eager and naive. A week later with their meager possessions, they boarded a bus. The excitement was palpable. And that was it. Instead of heading east to China, the bus barrelled south deep into Western Europe. The destination was a town in Germany where they were taken to an apartment, locked up and deprived of food and water. The girls' dreams quickly degenerated into a gruelling nightmare. They were yelled at constantly. Sometimes they were beaten. A few days later they were herded into a living room and ordered to disrobe in front of a group of men with bodyguards in tow. The thugs ogled the girls and began bidding, buying the orphans outright in lots of three, four and five. The girls were then distributed to various German brothels, where they were forced to have sex with up to ten men a day.

(Malarek 2004: 17)

Although horrific, this form of recruiting women into prostitution is at the extreme end of the spectrum. More often women become involved in a form of debt bondage either for a specific period of time or for life. The earnings of the women go towards the liquidation of the debt. During the period of debt bondage the woman is usually kept in a form of confinement, having their passports taken. In some cases there may be threats to the women or to their families about non-compliance. The women may be required to pay for food, lodging, clothing and shelter and the owner will aim to extend the period of debt bondage while the woman is young and attractive enough to attract clients. Liberal critics, however, claim that women often knowingly travel to other countries to engage in prostitution because it is seen as a better option than living in poverty at home (Agustin 2006).

However, Liz Kelly (2003) has suggested that to see the issue of trafficking primarily in relation to an opposition between force and free choice is to pose the issue in the wrong terms. Although she believes that sexual exploitation and human smuggling are serious problems throughout Europe, most trafficking she suggests is more mundane and it largely involves 'assisted migration' as well as forms of deception and debt bondage. Most poor women who migrate are unlikely to find their way into sex markets without facilitation. Consequently, few will arrive without considerable debts and obligations. In many cases women are deceived about what type of work they will be expected to undertake, for how long and in what conditions they will have to work. Strategically and politically Kelly argues that becoming embedded in a coercion/free choice dichotomy serves to legitimise inappropriate law enforcement campaigns and can inadvertently end up by rationalising the deportation of those who become involved in prostitution out of 'free choice'.

Thus although debt bondage and deception are prevalent, control over the prostitute is rarely total and long term. Within different sectors of the sex industry, women are able to exercise some autonomy and control and limit their level of unfreedom. The attention given to dramatic stories of abduction, however horrific they may be, mask the fact that many women willingly engage in 'trafficking' and may knowingly travel to other countries to engage in prostitution although the conditions they experience may be different than expected. The accounts which focus on stories of abduction and coercion, it is argued, draw on the myth of 'white slavery' which is centred around anxieties about female sexuality and women's' autonomy (Doezema 2000). The 'white slave' myth reinforces notions of female dependence and purity.

In his discussion of the international crusade against 'white slavery' at the end of the nineteenth century, Edward Bristow (1977) argued that this myth played upon the fears associated with the changing role of women, domestic and international migration and rapid urban redevelopment. He writes:

> In an age of female emancipation it was comforting for men to subscribe to the white slave myth, with its connotations of female helplessness, because it symbolised the simpler days before women demanded personal and political rights. As adolescents became the objects of increased social control it was natural for parents to give credence to the same myth ... Many reported that abductions and druggings were connected with contemporary novelties that had both frightening and stimulating facets, the dark cinema and the powerful motor car.
>
> (Bristow 1977: 189)

It should be noted that most brothel owners do not directly employ women but only charge admittance fees in order to avoid charges of 'living off immoral earnings' and may provide benefits and incentives. In many ways these self-employed women who work in brothels can exercise some control on the nature of their work even if it is the case that the brothel owners set the prices, the number of clients and the range of services provided (O'Connell-Davidson 1998; 2006).

Those women who work without pimps on the streets or from private flats engage in a form of prostitution which more closely resembles wage labour and they can exercise more choice over the number of clients, prices charged and services provided. In fact, most women involved in prostitution are neither subject to total control at one extreme or exercise total autonomy on the other, while some women can more effectively set limits on their unfreedom and experience a degree of independence.

Determining the degree of slavery involved in different forms of prostitution is an empirical question. Control is rarely absolute but can take a number of forms. However there are no doubt elements of slavery associated with most forms of prostitution since it necessarily involves the transfer of certain powers or commands over the person.

Conclusion

In this chapter the aim has been to identify some myths and misconceptions which have historically influenced and (mis)directed the debate. Related to these myths there are also a series of dichotomies and euphemisms that hinder and in some cases prevent constructive discussion of the issue. The ongoing dualisms which centre around whether those involved in prostitution are victims or offenders, are agents expressing free choice or whether prostitution represents violence against women, have created a form of polarisation which has trapped the debate in a series of unresolved dichotomies. In the course of the book the aim will be to work through some of these dualisms with the aim of developing a more realistic understanding of the issue (Matthews and Young 1992).

The debate has also become steeped in euphemisms. Those involved in prostitution are increasingly referred to as 'sex workers', brothels are generally referred to as 'massage parlours' and 'saunas', and pimps have become 'boyfriends'. The role of these euphemisms is to render the phenomena more opaque and serve to muddy the conceptual waters. The terms and categories that we use provide the conceptual lens through which we analyse phenomena. The problem with certain euphemisms is that they tend to cloud rather than clear the lens.

The history of prostitution is replete with euphemisms such as 'ladies of the night', 'fallen women', 'whores', 'scarlet ladies', 'harlots' as well as terms like 'punters' and 'johns' for those who pay for sex. 'Sex worker' is the latest in a series of euphemisms. Unlike previous euphemisms, however, the adoption of the term 'sex worker' involves the blurring of boundaries between a wide range of different activities that have varying relations to 'sex' and fails to distinguish between prostitution, pornographic work, stripping, telephone sex, hostessing and lap dancing and treats them all as if they were the same phenomena. The adoption of terms like 'sex work' is in fact a mode of distancing, sanitising and rationalising prostitution, which at once denies the specificity of prostitution in relation to other forms of sexual activity while failing to convey its uniqueness.

It is misleading to suggest that in the vast majority of encounters involving prostitution that the woman is supplying 'sex' in the conventional sense of the term. What she provides, at best, is a fantasy or a projection of the clients sexual desires and interests. In the vast majority of cases she is acting out a role. She has little or no sexual interest in the encounter and her aim is to get it over with as quickly as possible. She is not doing 'sex'. The term 'work' is also not entirely appropriate in this context, as has been suggested, because of its exceptional and unique nature it does not simply involve the normal processes of selling one's labour power in the market in an impersonal way. Rather, it involves selling an intimate part of oneself from which it is extremely difficult, if not impossible, to disassociate oneself. Thus, as has been suggested, it is a very unique and exceptional activity and therefore not a form of work like any other. The term 'sex work' is apparently the invention of agency workers and activists who claim to represent prostitutes. However, the euphemism which many of those involved in prostitution seem to prefer is 'working women'. In general, this seems to be a more appropriate and neutral term than 'sex worker' (Leigh 1997).

It is also argued that 'sex worker' is a less stigmatising term than 'prostitute' and that it is non-essentialist. Unlike the term 'working women' the term 'sex worker' carries strong connotations of trading in sex and therefore given our cultural norms has considerable stigmatising potential. It defines the women in relation to 'sex' and it is in this respect no more or less essentialising than the term 'prostitute'. However, the term 'sex worker' has now taken on a political significance and it is the term of preference amongst liberals, neo-liberals and libertarians. Thus using this term does not so much describe a specific phenomena as reflect a particular political orientation.

The term 'prostitute' is used as we have noted by some of the older prostitutes rights groups like the English Collective of Prostitutes and in many parts of the world it is the term which is most commonly used to describe women involved in prostitution, although as Sheila Jeffreys (1997) points out the term 'prostitute' itself is deficient in that it implies that prostitution is a function of the activities of the 'prostitute' while omitting reference to those who pay for sex. It can, all too easily, become a form of 'victim blaming' by deflecting attention away from the client while reinforcing the double standard, which holds women responsible for prostitution. Like other radical feminists Jeffreys prefers to refer to 'prostituted women' rather than prostitutes because it emphasises the dependent position of the woman and her lack of choice. But this terminology only perpetuates rather than resolves the free choice/coercion dichotomy. Having suggested that the free choice/coercion dualism is unhelpful the phrase 'women involved in prostitution' will be mainly used throughout this book as it is seen to be both more accurate and less essentialising than the alternative terminology. Using this phrase is designed to establish some distance from both the 'sex work' liberals on one side and radical feminists on the other.

Chapter 3

Prostitution, vulnerability and victimisation

Introduction

Historically, the female prostitute has been cast as the offender, the deviant, the violator of sexual norms, the transmitter of disease and has consequently become the principle object of regulation. Only when prostitutes are young, overtly coerced, or treated like slaves have they elicited any sympathy as victims. However, over the past decade the perception of the female prostitute has begun to change significantly and she is coming, in the UK at least, to be seen as being more sinned against than sinning. Thus, until fairly recently female prostitutes were subject to a combination of criminal justice and medical interventions which have involved different forms of policing, surveillance, fines, inspection and detention. However, in the current period there is a growing emphasis on providing help and support for those involved in prostitution.

Although some of the diverse control strategies remain in force while other modes of regulation have to some extent expanded and intensified there can be little doubt that the public and political conception of 'the prostitute' in the UK and in other countries is changing. This development is a function of a number of changing lines of force. First, the level and range of victimisation experienced by many prostitutes is being reported in more detail as research studies on prostitution proliferate. Second, and relatedly, the growing focus on 'trafficking' and the disturbing media accounts which have detailed the levels of coercion and abuse which some of these women experience has brought the vulnerability of poor but 'respectable' women to the attention of the general public. Even in situations in which women are not overtly coerced, the high visibility of an increasing number of foreign women involved in prostitution, has drawn attention to the level of desperation and poverty which has driven these women to travel to foreign destinations to earn money in the sex industry.

Third, the growth of prostitute support groups who are becoming increasingly active politically at both the local and national level have done a great deal to humanise the female prostitute and encourage a more sympathetic response to their situation. Fourth, a growing body of radical feminists have increasingly come to depict the female prostitute as the victim in need of welfare and protection from the ravages of male violence and exploitation (Barry 1995; Jeffreys 1997). However, possibly the most significant development in the UK in recent years has been the increased visibility on the streets of women suffering from drug addiction, problems of physical and mental health and the sight of an increasing number of women who appear extremely desperate, damaged and disorganised.

As suggested above, it was the case that 20 or 30 years ago in the urban centres in Britain that the majority of women were motivated by economic pressures to work as prostitutes. Although some of these women may have been drug users or have consumed large amounts of alcohol they appeared to have a certain level of personal organisation, competence and control. However, due to increased community pressure, more intensive forms of policing, increased concerns about violence and the like many of these 'economic' prostitutes – particularly those who engaged in prostitution on a more temporary paid or sporadic basis – have either found alternative ways to make a living or have left prostitution prematurely. There has also been a decrease in recent years of the number of young girls entering and remaining in prostitution. The net result of the developments is that an increasing proportion of those left working on the street are drug dependent women who experience a range of victimisation and are increasingly recognised as a vulnerable group in need of intensive forms of care and support.

As the level and the impact of the victimisation experienced by many of those women currently involved in prostitution has become much more systematically documented through research, public and political attitudes have begun to change. While most of the research to date has focused on the victimisation of those who work on the street there is a growing body of evidence that suggests that many of the women who work off-street are also subject to forms of victimisation, although the nature and degree of victimisation tends to be different (Dickson 2004; Sanders 2005).

Not all prostitutes are subject to the same forms of victimisation. The nature and intensity of victimisation will depend upon the form of prostitution in which they are involved. However, it is difficult to find a group whose experience of victimisation is more continuous or concentrated than that of women involved in prostitution, particularly those who work on the street. The impact of victimisation is in many cases cumulative and occurs repeatedly over a period of time.

In the broadest terms, the majority of female prostitutes can be considered victims of poverty and deprivation, on the one hand, and a sexual ideology which sees the female as 'supplying' sex in order to satisfy male sexual desires, on the other. Although there are some exceptions the vast majority of the women who engage in prostitution do it to earn the money to buy things they need whether it is food, drugs or to pay household bills. Thus, it is a reasonable to hypothesise that in those communities with a high level of welfare provision, a reasonable minimum wage, a relatively generous system of unemployment benefits, child care facilities and allowances, that the proportion of indigenous women involved in prostitution will be low. By the same token, those communities with high levels of poverty, minimal welfare and support systems and a double standard of sexual morality will tend to have relatively high levels of indigenous prostitution.

There are a number of forms of victimisation associated with involvement in prostitution. Many of those involved in prostitution have a history of abuse, neglect and marginalisation. These forms of abuse and neglect tend to be replicated through the life course in different forms. It has been estimated, for example, that experience of child abuse doubles or even trebles the risk of sexual re-victimisation for adult women (Classen et al. 2005; Tyler et al. 2000). Also, we know in general that the one of the best predictors of future victimisation is previous victimisation (Farrell and Pease 1993).

Housing is a critical, but often neglected, issue for a significant proportion of women involved in prostitution. Homelessness, or living in temporary accommodation has been found to be common both at the point of entering prostitution and subsequently. One study carried out in London, for example, found that just over half of those interviewed were either homeless, living in a hostel or serving a prison sentence. The level of homelessness was found to be highest amongst the younger respondents (Cusick, Martin and May 2003). The San Francisco study by Farley and Barkan (1998) found that 84 per cent of those interviewed reported current or past homelessness.

The range and regularity of victimisation, which many of the women involved in prostitution experience, is daunting. Victimisation at times appears to be continuous and relentless. It is often built into the fabric of the women's lives. Although the range and impact of victimisation experienced by these women is extensive the main focus of this chapter will be on violence and coercion, drug use and physical and mental health.

Violence and coercion

For most of the women who work on the streets in the UK the reality and the threat of violence is of constant concern. Violence comes predominantly from male clients on the one hand and pimps on the other. It also occasionally comes from other prostitutes. It mainly takes the form of physical violence and threats but can also involve emotional and psychological abuse. In general, the high level of violence directed at female prostitutes is seen to be a function of differential gender socialisation, vulnerability and the impunity that many perpetrators feel that they have when carrying out acts of violence against those involved in prostitution (McKeganey and Barnard 1996).

The data compiled through the Home Office-funded Crime Reduction Programme (CRP) found that of the 140 women in the sample, three quarters had experienced physical violence. In one study carried out in Merseyside, it was found that just over half the women had been physically assaulted, while a third had been raped (Campbell 2002). In addition, 43 per cent of the women interviewed had been threatened with a weapon and 13 per cent had been abducted. In six out of 10 cases the perpetrators were either kerb crawlers or pimps. Another study included within the CRP programme which was based on interviews with 133 women, found that just over half of the women had been forced to have sex or had been indecently assaulted. Over half of the women in the CRP survey said they had feared for their lives at least once (Hester and Westmarland 2004). One American study found that while a certain amount of violence is perpetuated by clients that most prostitution-related violence arises from encounters between prostitutes and their pimps (Dalla 2002). In general, however, the level of violence is reported to be considerably higher for those women who work on the street than those who work indoors. Church et al. (2001) found that women working on the street were subject to six times the level of violence than those working indoors. Significantly, only one in three of those who had experienced violence reported it to the police.

Violence, it would seem for the majority of the more vulnerable street workers, is part of their everyday lives. Some 60 prostitutes have been murdered in the UK since 1990 and although these high profile cases receive some media and police attention the everyday routine level of serious violence directed at those involved in prostitution goes largely unnoticed. It is the range, seriousness and frequency of violence against those involved in prostitution that is so disturbing. Interviews with individual women provide a series of graphic accounts of the long-term experience of violence. One woman who worked in Wolverhampton summarised her experiences:

> I've had clients try to rape me, try to strangle me, took off with me in the car where I have had to climb out of the window and the car's been 90 miles an hour . . . jumped out of the car at 40 miles an hour. I've had a client shoot me with a starting gun but I thought it was a real gun . . . I've had them try to run me over and everything. I've had them attack me because they wanted their money back because they have ejaculated too quick, else they haven't been satisfied, or I've says 'look your time's up' and they want more time but they don't want to pay the extra money – things like that. And I have had clients attack me because other girls are robbing them.
>
> (Boynton 1998: 24)

All of the women working on the streets in the UK could probably provide similar accounts of their experiences. There is also, no doubt, some who have left prostitution as a result of the violence directed towards them. All of the women in the Wolverhampton survey had experienced high levels of violence from clients as well as from pimps and partners. What is remarkable about this situation is that despite the continuous nature of the violence directed at street prostitutes many continue working. There can be no other occupation where the risks and experiences of interpersonal violence are so pronounced and the level of protection so limited.

American research has found similar levels and patterns of violence, although higher levels of serious violence against those working indoors has been reported than studies carried out in the UK (Sanders 2005). These differences may be to do with differences of methodology and theoretical orientation as well as cultural variations. In one study in San Francisco, for example, 80 per cent of those of 130 women involved in street prostitution had been physically assaulted and 68 per cent had been raped (Farley and Barkan 1998). Research conducted in New Zealand examined the experiences of those working indoors and on the street and found that 41 per cent of street workers reported assaults compared to 21 per cent of indoor workers. Also, 27 per cent of street workers reported having been raped compared to 8 per cent of those working off street (Plumridge and Abel 2001).

While it is generally the case that that the level of violence directed against those who work on the streets is higher than that directed to those who work indoors, a number of American studies have reported significant levels of violence directed at those who work off street. Moreover, one Canadian study reported that 56 per cent of respondents stated that they had been hospitalised specifically for injuries they had incurred while working indoors (Benoit and Millar 2001). Similarly, a study in Chicago involving 222 women working both on street and off street, found that while those working on the street experienced the most serious and consistent levels of violence, that over half of the women providing escort services reported forced sex and high levels of rape; while a third of those working from flats reported experiencing at least one form of sexual violence – threatened rape, fingers or objects inserted vaginally, or forced sex. The largest group of perpetrators were the clients, although one quarter of respondents had experienced violence at the hands of their partners, while just over a third who were victims of forced sex identified a pimp as the perpetrator (Raphael and Shapiro 2004). The conclusion of this study is that serious physical and sexual assault is more common against those who work off street than is often assumed and the depiction of the indoor sex trade as a harmless form of consensual entertainment may be an illusion.

It is almost certainly the case that the levels of violence both among women who work on the streets and those working indoors is probably even higher than the research suggests. Because those involved in prostitution feel that their reports will not be taken seriously or because of their own quasi-legal status women are reluctant to report incidents. This is more likely to be the case in relation to violence perpetrated by pimps and partners. If more of these incidents are to be reported and acted upon prostitutes need to feel assured that action will be taken and offenders prosecuted. While prostitutes continue to be identified as offenders rather than victims, the likelihood is that the violence directed at them will continue and their willingness to report will not increase.

Drug use

It has been noted above that there is a long historical association between drug use and prostitution. The major change, in recent years, however, is the type of drugs and the proportion of street prostitutes who are problematic drug users. A number of commentators have identified this shift towards the injection of heroin as well as an increase in the use of crack cocaine. In some areas of the UK, the percentage of women working on the streets who are identified as problematic drug users is as high as 60–90 per cent (Church et al. 2001; McKeganey 2006).

In some urban areas the visible signs of drug addiction amongst women working on the street are both highly visible and disturbing. In Glasgow, for example, it was reported that:

> It was not difficult to see the visible signs of such widespread drug use among the women. On virtually every night of our fieldwork there were women working who could barely stand up and who would either stagger from street to street or lean precariously against one of the buildings waiting for a client to drive by.
>
> (McKeganey and Barnard 1996: 44)

The authors note that a number of the women were 'out of their skulls', whilst there were others who could barely stand or speak. They note that despite their appearance and condition, that there was no shortage of clients picking up such women. Indeed, they suggest, that it may be that certain clients are attracted by the vulnerability of these women, although these women did not have 'sufficient consciousness to know what they were doing'. The heavier the use of drugs the more likely it is that the women will work for longer hours, for less money and in some cases it may reduce the likelihood of condom use.

The changing patterns and level of drug use has affected the composition of women working on the street. It also arguably, makes these women more vulnerable and less likely to practice safe sex. Drug use for many of these women sets the pace and determines the intensity of their activities. The price of a 'rock' or a 'hit' can determine the number of clients serviced in a day and the prices charged. Those who are most desperate may be willing to lower prices or perform services that they otherwise would not be willing to offer.

Street prostitutes frequently report that they work to support not only their own habit but also that of their boyfriend, pimp or partner. In some cases male drug users/dealers will seek out female prostitutes as 'partners' since they make good customers and providers. The increased use of crack cocaine among street-based prostitutes has had particularly profound effects on this part of the sex trade. Philip Bourgois (2003) has suggested that crack cocaine is the preferred drug of abuse among 'desperate populations and subgroups that are victims of extreme forms of structural violence'. In America in the 1990s the use of crack cocaine was concentrated among poor African Americans and Puerto Ricans living in predominantly ghetto areas (Bourgois 2002). It is no accident, he argues, that crack came to be used in this period and he suggests that 'social and economic predictors of crack cocaine use are high levels of economic exploitation, systematic discrimination and spatial and social segregation'. He notes that:

Crack is so destructive pharmacologically to individuals who use it chronically that it self regulates itself to shorter cycles of addiction then to less physically and emotionally destructive drugs such as marijuana or even opiates and benzodiazepines. Although very different from a pharmacological perspective from angel dust, crack is perhaps comparable to that drug from a social perspective because of the destructiveness of lifestyle.

(Bourgois 2002: 33)

Bourgois makes an important distinction between the psychological impact of drug use and the social effects. The significance of crack cocaine is that it is destructive on both levels simultaneously. He also notes that a disproportionate number of crack addicts are what he describes as 'throwaways'. That is, individuals who have suffered abuse and neglect in their family life.

As in the research on violence, the available research on drugs suggests that the level of problematic drug use tends to be more prevalent amongst those who work on the streets than those who work indoors. Recent research in the UK, for example, has found that only 6 per cent of indoor workers report using heroin, 5 per cent crack cocaine and 4 per cent reported injecting in the six months prior to interview (Church et al. 2001; Cusick and Hickman 2005). However, it would be misleading from these figures to conclude that the level of drug use and drug addiction is not part of the indoor sex industry, since other research suggests that many of those who work indoors are regular or even heavy drug users, but that they tend to use a different combination of drugs. May and Hunter (2000), for example, found that 79 per cent of those working off-street had used tranquilisers and 30 per cent had used amphetamines in the previous six months prior to interview. These differences in the patterns of drug use between street prostitutes and those who work indoors may reflect the different social demographic characteristics and personal backgrounds of the women who work in these different locations. Also, the entrepreneurs who run brothels and escort agencies are unlikely to employ workers who are visibly drug addicted because they are seen as unreliable and difficult to manage. Consequently, those women who work in brothels who are regular drug users are unlikely to reveal this aspect of their lives to researchers.

American research has found a close relationship between drug use and violence. This may be a function on one hand of the greater vulnerability of those addicted to drugs, while the use of certain drugs such as crack cocaine tends to increase instability and aggression on the part of the user (Sterk and Elifson 1990; Dalla 2002). Thus, as the level of problematic drug use increases among street prostitutes it is likely to increase the vulnerability of the whole group, not just those individuals who are problematic drug users.

A significant percentage of the prostitutes only become problematic drug users after becoming involved in prostitution. For others, their level of their drug use has intensified in order to deal with the demands and pressures of their work. Apart from 'trapping' many of these women into prostitution the use of drugs tends to increase their vulnerability and can have serious adverse effects on their mental and physical health.

Mental and physical health

Many occupations are associated with health problems whether it is to do with stress, pollution or exhaustion. Prostitution is no exception in this regard, except in relation to the type and intensity of the risks involved. Many of those who have entered prostitution at a young age are already victims of abuse and neglect and consequently a significant number are damaged physically and emotionally even before they expose themselves to the considerable health risks associated with involvement in prostitution. The major problem is while these childhood experiences provide an ideal preparation for entry into prostitution, that once these young people become involved in prostitution these problems are likely to increase and intensify.

No doubt many prostitutes devise imaginative and ingenious methods for coping with the strains and demands of prostitution (Phoenix 1999). But whatever rationalisations they, and various commentators place on their activities, there can be little doubt that entry into prostitution increases their victimisation and vulnerability. Hoigard and Finstad (1992) have outlined some of the coping strategies that street prostitutes typically develop to manage their situations. Prostitutes, they suggest, make distinction between their public and private lives, turning off all emotions, restricting access to certain parts of their bodies, limiting intimacy and getting the transaction over with as quickly as possible.

The high percentage of women who are problematic drug users has direct and indirect implications for physical and mental health. At one extreme there is a very real danger of death and disease from using dirty needles and contaminated products. At the other extreme, the frequent use of drugs such as crack cocaine can have a damaging impact over time on the mental and physical state of users. Being continually 'high' when working makes women vulnerable and more likely to be victims of assaults, rape and abuse. Many of the drug dependent women on the street are undernourished and under-weight and reports by health specialists make continual reference to the generally poor health of women involved in prostitution (Day 2007). In one London-based survey covering three boroughs it was reported that:

> Employees of these kinds of health services in the three boroughs listed a range of health consequences demonstrably associated with chaotic life-styles. Some of these may be direct effects of sex work or substance use. Others are more directly related to homelessness, vulnerability and prob-lematic drug use. They include a high prevalence of STIs and Hepatitis C, injecting related abscesses and infections, problems with the upper respiratory tract as a result of crack use, risk of heart attack as a result of crack use, dietary problems as a result of not eating properly, colds caused by rough sleeping and constant exposure to elements (to include pneumonia), and sleep deprivation.
>
> (Nash et al. 2004: 30)

The cumulative nature of these ailments, which are to a large extent associ-ated with involvement in prostitution, is that they can have a devastating effect in the medium and long term on the health of these women. Because of homelessness or the chaotic lifestyles of many street based prostitutes they are unlikely to be registered with health services and their treatment tends to be more sporadic. There are also harms associated with frequent sexual activ-ity in relation to infertility, high levels of sexually transmitted diseases, par-ticularly gonorrhoea and pelvic inflammatory disease. A recent longitudinal study which examined the health and career paths of 130 women in the UK over 15 years concluded that: 'sex work is associated with excess mortality and morbidity including the sequence of STI, mental health problems and substance abuse' (Ward and Day 2006). A similar set of problems was reported in Farley and Barkan's (1998) study in San Francisco with half of those interviewed stating that they had a physical health problem. These health problems included arthritis (14%) cardiovascular symptoms (12%) liver disorders (10%) and a further 9 per cent reported respiratory symptoms.

Another American study conducted by Potterat et al. (2004) estimated that among a cohort of just under 2,000 female prostitutes working in Colorado that the mortality rate was 18 times greater than for non-prostitute women of the same age. The same study found that the leading causes of death were homicide (19%), drug ingestions (18%) accidents (12%) and alcohol-related causes (9%). The mortality rate was significantly higher among women work-ing on the street. This finding coincides with the findings from the UK which shows that 84 per cent of known prostitutes who have been murdered worked on the streets (Kinnell 2006).

Young people involved in prostitution: from offenders to victims

One of the most remarkable developments in the field of crime control is when a group changes their status from offenders to victims. This is precisely what happened to young people involved in prostitution in the UK in the 1990s. In fact, during the second half of the 1990s a sea change occurred whereby young people involved in prostitution were no longer seen as wilful offenders, but were increasingly viewed as victims of abuse.

This change of attitude and intervention appears to be a function of a growing national and international interest in defending the rights of children, limiting sexual exploitation, and reducing the involvement of children in pornography and prostitution. At the same time, the failures of the child welfare system in general and the detrimental impact of being placed in local authority care, in particular, have become more widely recognised.

The Children Act 1989 signalled a growing official interest in child protection and a number of official publications appeared over the next two decades that expressed a commitment to safeguarding and promoting the welfare of all children 'in need' or 'at risk' of engaging in prostitution (Department of Health 2001; Green 1992; Levy 2004; London Assembly 2005; Scott and Skidmore 2006). There was also a commitment to tackle child abuse and to deal with its effects. In particular, there has been a growing interest in preventing young people becoming involved in prostitution, as well as growing efforts to prosecute those who coerce, exploit or abuse young people (Shaw and Butler 1998).

Local Area Child Protection Committees (LACPCs) have been set up in England. They include representatives from the police, social services, voluntary organisations, youth services, probation and other agencies. The aim of this inter-agency group has been to encourage a systematic and comprehensive welfare-based approach to youth prostitution (Swann and Balding 2002; Phoenix 2002). Thus, whereas in the early 1990s young people involved in prostitution were regularly prosecuted, by the end of the decade a more welfarist approach was being advocated in official circles. In one influential report published by the Department of Health the authors state that: 'children who are involved in prostitution are exposed to abuse and assault. It deprives them of their childhood; it may even threaten their lives and certainly causes them long term harm' (Swann and Balding 2002: 3).

In conjunction with these official publications were a number of other publications produced by organisations like the Children's Society and Barnardo's that documented the negative consequences of young people being involved in prostitution. The Barnardo's publication 'Stolen

Childhood', for example, included graphic accounts of the detrimental effects of prostitution on young people (Palmer and Stacey 2002). Backed up by growing evidence of abuse and exploitation, these organisations have been able to help transform how young people involved or 'at risk' of becoming involved in prostitution are perceived (Ayre and Barrett 2000).

These and other campaigning organisations have managed to convey the message that these are not 'child prostitutes' but rather victims of abuse and even rape. Because they are not in a position to offer informed consent they are, by definition, unable to engage in a contractual relationship and consequently their position is always one of dependency, abuse and exploitation. In some areas, there were reports of young girls being sought out and of particular punters targeting underage girls. These individuals are seen not so much as punters but as child sex abusers/offenders (Swann and Baldwin 2002).

Significantly, the campaigns to transform the status of young people involved in prostitution in England and Wales from offenders to victims was not orchestrated by the growing numbers of 'sex work' support groups who by and large took a 'non-judgemental' approach and thereby observed and in many cases facilitated this form of 'child abuse' by providing support services that were designed to keep these young people 'on the game'. It was the major child support agencies, radical academics and a few progressive politicians who spearheaded this campaign and brought attention to this issue, ultimately changing public and political perceptions.

Treating adult prostitutes as victims

To have suggested 10 or 15 years ago that we treat adults involved in prostitution as victims rather than offenders would have produced derision and disbelief. However, a number of developments have taken place, which not only makes such a conception plausible but indeed necessary.

The dramatic transformation in the way that the involvement in prostitution of those under 18 has been perceived over the last decade, is testimony of the possibility of changing from offender to victim status in a relatively short period of time. It is estimated that some 60 to 70 per cent of those adults who are currently engaged in street prostitution in the UK first became involved under the age of 18 (May et al. 1999; Hester and Westmarland 2004). Thus, many of these women would have qualified for victim status during their early years of involvement in prostitution but once they have passed their 18th birthday they surprisingly are no longer eligible. In some cases this may be because the period of time that they have been involved in prostitution has been extended as they have become trapped by a series of processes. Although many of these 'adults' will have had their childhoods taken away from them they are deemed at the age of 18 to suddenly make informed choices. In some cases they may at 18 be more dependent, more unable to make rational and informed choices and suffer greater levels of victimisation than at any previous point in their lives. The attribution of victim status, therefore, should be more closely tied to the *competence* of the women concerned as well as their age.

Within the current policy, the implication is that once these girls pass the age of 18 their previous histories and experiences somehow evaporate or are no longer relevant (Jeffreys 2000). It is as if a form of amnesia sets in as they reach their 18th birthday and all their previous histories melt into air. In many ways these adult women can be seen as the victims of inadequate state intervention, which has been unable and unwilling to provide the necessary support to take them out of prostitution when they were younger. They are also in a number of cases the victims of the institutions in which they have been placed, as well as victims of a failed welfare system that was unable to respond to their predicament and instead criminalised their actions.

It might be argued that the transformation of young people involved in prostitution from offenders to victims only occurred because society has recently developed a more positive and sympathetic view of young people. In some respect this may be true, but the logic of the arguments which were put forward in the 1990s in relation to child prostitution is in many ways equally applicable to adults. Many adults involved in prostitution continue to experience forms of abuse, violence and coercion as well as degrees of exploitation. A consistent and comprehensive approach to prostitution would have to apply similar considerations to adult prostitutes as to those which are currently afforded to young people involved in prostitution.

There are some signs, however, that adult prostitutes in the UK are coming to be seen more as victims than offenders. The first indication is that the number of women convicted or arrested for soliciting in England and Wales has fallen sharply over the past decade. In 1992, 12,896 women were either cautioned or found guilty of soliciting-related offences at Magistrates' courts. By 2002 this number had fallen to just over 3,000 (Matthews 2005).

Interviews with the police, who in the past have been largely responsible for regulating prostitution, indicate that a more tolerant and sympathetic approach has developed in the last decade with the police increasingly referring those involved in prostitution to support, welfare and drug agencies rather than arresting them (Matthews 2005). With the shift towards an inter-agency or a 'partnership' approach the police have been willing to broaden the framework of regulation, taking less direct responsibility themselves for controlling prostitution (Scoular and O'Neill 2007). The growth of specialist prostitute support agencies has been an important factor in this process. Increasingly, these agencies are taking a central role at the local level in finding solutions to problems associated with prostitution. In general, there are a number of signs that attitudes to those women who work on the streets are changing and they are increasingly being seen as victims rather than offenders, being more in need of welfare and support than punishment.

Victimisation and the off-street trade

Although the research evidence, to date, indicates that those who work on the street are subject to more intense and systematic forms of victimisation than those who work off street, it may well be the case that the level of victimisation experienced by those who work off street may be significantly higher than is currently acknowledged. In many respects the clandestine and less visible nature of off street prostitution deflects attention from the victimisation experienced by women working in brothels or other premises. While it has been noted above that women working indoors experience a significant level of violence and that many are frequent drug users, the form of victimisation that these women experience tends to be less visible and more subtle.

The proliferation of off-street prostitution in the UK has gone largely unrecorded (Matthews 1997). However, a recent study conducted by the Poppy Project in London found that every London borough has premises used for prostitution and, in all, 730 sites were identified in London. Thus, for example, every high street in London now has a brothel masquerading as a 'sauna' or a 'massage parlour' involving between 3,000 and 6,000 women. These establishments employ mainly foreign women from Eastern Europe, South East Asia and Africa who, because of their language or status problems, are highly vulnerable and are often unable to access services. In interviews, trafficked women:

> described meeting women who were held under varying degrees of control, from giving all their earnings to their pimp trafficker and being escorted to and from work. However, some of the women said that they had some degree of control over their money and their personal freedom. Some witnessed other trafficked women being physically beaten and less frequently stabbed for resisting their pimp/trafficker. Some were locked into flats when other trafficked women escaped.
>
> (Dickson 2004: 20)

Many of the foreign women working as prostitutes in the UK have been deceived, pressured or misled about the type of work they would have to do and the length of time the would have to do it for. In most of these establishments the women who work there have little or no choice over customers and are often required to perform sexual services whether they want to or not. This is the case for both trafficked or non-trafficked women. It is also reported that many women working in 'saunas' and 'massage parlours' or flats are encouraged to have unprotected sex, while little is done to support or identify the needs of these women.

The police response to the off-street trade in the UK is decidedly low-key. Although brothels are illegal, the police generally turn a blind eye to the operation of these establishments, while local authorities continue to licence them as bona fide saunas and massage parlours. Everybody over the age of 12, however, knows that these establishments are brothels – except apparently for the people that work in the local authority licensing departments (Benson and Matthews 2000).

It is only when there is an incident reported to the police or where there is a report of brothels using underage girls that the police tend to intervene. There have, however, been a few examples recently of interventions directed at off-street premises. In 2004, for example, the police were involved in a major investigation into trafficking in Yorkshire, which lasted over 18 months and involved 300 staff. Operation Rampart, as it was called, investigated the role of organised crime, the involvement of foreign women and illegal immigrants as well as juveniles. Eleven men were arrested for 'living off immoral proceeds' and 47 women were arrested and deported despite the police claiming that they viewed them as 'victims'. The brothels were closed and approximately £1.5 million was seized in assets.

Another recent initiative by West Midlands Police in 2000 resulted in a raid on a brothel in Birmingham and the 'rescue' of 19 foreign women who were thought to have been tricked into becoming prostitutes. Two people were arrested and assets were seized but despite the fact that the women were locked in all day in these establishments and treated like slaves they were still deported.

In London, the Metropolitan Police Vice Unit conducted operation 'Kon Tiki' in 2004. This initiative involved gathering information on London's brothels from women working in these establishments. One outcome of this investigation was the imprisonment of one Albanian sex trafficker for 11 years and the deportation of his younger brother. In 2006 Operation Pentameter was launched to tackle the illegal exploitation of trafficking victims, whilst targetting organised criminals. To date, 525 premises have been raided, 88 victims recovered and 232 arrests have been made.

A number of raids have also been carried out by the Clubs and Vice Unit, which have resulted in the arrest and deportation of a number of foreign women working in brothels. The Sexual Offences Act 2003 and the Immigration, Asylum and Nationality Act 2006 have made prosecutions easier although the response remains too fragmented and inconsistent. Another police initiative has called for male clients to report in confidence cases where they believe women working in brothels have been trafficked. A similar initiative has also been developed in Holland (Red Thread 2006).

These initiatives, although well intentioned, are too infrequent and are largely reactive. A more proactive intelligence based strategy which treats foreign women as victims needs to be developed since the off-street trade is expanding apace and the exploitation of those involved in prostitution is by all accounts increasing while the police response remains extremely limited (Kelly and Regan 2003).

Victims and victimhood

There is considerable resistance amongst those writing on prostitution to see those involved in prostitution as victims. This antipathy stems in part from an ongoing debate in feminist theory about seeing women as 'victims', since it is argued that such a categorisation essentialises, stigmatises and pathologises women while stripping them of agency.

Because of the potentially stigmatising connotations of being identified as a victim some writers prefer to use the term 'survivor' which they feel is less prejudicial (Davis 2000). However, the term 'survivor' suggests an ongoing passivity and is no less essentialising than the term 'victim'.

The claim that women involved in prostitution are subject to a range of victimisation does not render them passive or deny agency. As victimologists have pointed out many of those who become victims are complicit in their victimisation and carry some degree of 'responsibility' for their victimisation (Zedner 1997). In the language of victimology some people become victims because of 'victim precipitation'. That is, they 'choose' to place themselves at risk and in certain cases actively engage in certain forms of risk-taking activity. Those that leave their keys in the car, or leave their house windows open when they are out, are generally seen to carry some responsibility for their victimisation. Moreover, being a victim can generate a range of responses including both fear and anger (Ditton et al. 1999). The experience of victimisation therefore does not necessarily signify passivity but can be the basis for mobilisation and resistance. In relation to domestic violence, for example, we accept that women are routinely victims but this label of 'victim' does not deny agency. In some cases agency might mean taking defensive action while in others victims 'act' by deciding not to any action at all against the perpetrators (Kelly 2003).

Anyone who has conducted interviews with those involved in prostitution knows how resilient and resourceful that they can be. At the same time, however, those that have carried out research with street prostitutes in the UK cannot remain ignorant to the fact that many of the women are damaged, disorganised and vulnerable. To recognise these issues is not necessarily to pathologise the women involved. To deny or minimise the level of victimisation, however, would be a serious mistake and be a major disservice to the women concerned. The denial of victimisation undermines the development of internal and external controls to deal with victimisation (Pease 2008). The development of such controls are necessary if victimisation is to be reduced. Thus, instead of downplaying victimisation we need to encourage women to become more active in preventing future victimisation.

Just as we are caught to some extent in the problem of essentialism we are also caught in the victim-offender dichotomy. Unfortunately, there is not a hybrid category victim/offender and in everyday language victims and offenders are identified as mutually exclusive groups. For the most part the categorisation of people as victims or offenders is a function of the perceived balance between voluntarism and compulsion. Acquiring victim status arises from recognition of the forces in play which impact negatively on individuals and groups as well as recognising their degree of vulnerability. The identification of a powerful perpetrator who directs or controls the 'victim' adds weight to the victim status. The problem is that prostitutes are seen socially as a problematic group and therefore it is difficult to treat them in completely non-judgemental terms. Thus, in the current context to deny the victim the status of adult prostitutes would be to maintain their existing categorisation as offenders. There is no neutral or hybrid form of categorisation. Thus those who present ostensibly radical critiques of the recent government policy, that has come to identify young people involved in prostitution as victims of abuse, provide in effect a conservative defence of the status quo (Phoenix 2002).

In many respects, the victimisation of those involved in prostitution is predictable. Criminologists have explained how certain groups are more prone to victimisation than others. In a classic study by Richard Sparks (1981) on victimisation he claimed that there are six ways in which the actions, attributes and the social situations of individuals can help to explain variations in victimisation rates. These include 'precipitation' which involves acting in a way as to encourage the offender's behaviour; 'facilitation' by which the victim places themselves at risk; 'vulnerability' which implies that they are less than normally capable of protecting themselves; 'opportunity' which is of course a logically necessary condition; 'attractiveness' of the individual as a target for the offender and finally 'impunity' by which the offender feels that s/he has little chance of being caught or that the victim is unlikely to report the incident.

While Sparks' typology contains an element of victim blaming he does not see the victim as passive. Indeed rather than being passive, Sparks recognises that certain people will expose themselves to greater risks and to different forms of victimisation. Thus for Sparks and other victimologists identifying someone as a victim does not involve the denial of agency. Rather, where certain attributes combine, victimisation is predicted to be high and we can see in the case of street prostitutes that individually and collectively they are likely to score very highly in nearly all of these criteria.

However, in some respects, the women involved in prostitution do not constitute 'ideal victims'. As Nils Christie (1986), has argued, not all individuals or groups are readily identified as 'legitimate' victims. The location of many of the women involved in prostitution within the 'grey economy', their marginalised status, their reportedly high earnings, and lack of social and economic contribution to the community, disqualifies them in the eyes of many observers from claiming the status of 'legitimate' or 'ideal' victims. Christie argues that 'ideal victims' are the weak, the sick, the young and the very old. The 'ideal victim' needs to be engaged in a respectable project, exercise no choice about the location or situation in which the victimisation takes place and is unknown to the offender. Ideal victims, Christie argues, need ideal offenders. Ideal offenders need to be dangerous, brutal, preferably psychopaths. While the clients of prostitutes have in some cases perverse and unusual desires and readily resort to violence and intimidation the faceless nature of 'punters' and the widespread belief that they are sad and lonely men seeking sexual relief does not place them squarely in the frame as ideal offenders. On these criteria the female prostitute does not score very highly. However, as Christie notes, groups who do not necessarily meet all criteria for being considered an 'ideal victim' can still have their victimisation viewed sympathetically (Richardson and May 1999). Thus is precisely what has happened in the case of child prostitution.

Despite this qualification of the victim status of street prostitutes, recognition of the extent and impact of victimisation is necessary if we are to limit the experience of victimisation amongst this group. A number of important studies have been conducted in recent years to address different forms of victimisation, particularly related to drugs and violence from clients. Recent government documents have increasingly come to see all street prostitutes as victims to some degree. Much of the focus has been on young people but increasingly the victimisation experienced by adult prostitutes is coming to be recognised.

In sum, what is significant about the women involved in prostitution is that their victimisation is both extensive and continuous, particularly among those who work on the street. They are repeat victims and multiple victims. That is, they suffer the same forms of victimisation again and again and are also subject to a number of different forms of victimisation. Victimisation is therefore compounded, continuous and concentrated. It would be difficult to find a group who experience a greater and more diverse degree of victimisation than prostitutes. If the status of 'victim' is to have any meaning then street prostitutes, in particular, must qualify.

Conclusion

It is evident that entry into prostitution compounds and extends previous forms of victimisation. In this chapter the main forms of victimisation which have been identified are violence, drug use, housing and health issues. The forms of victimisation which many young people involved in prostitution experience has belatedly become recognised in official circles. However, when these same women reach 18 years of age the previous forms of victimisation are magically erased. Despite the fact that most of these forms of victimisation are continuous and in some cases increasing, the authorities continue to treat those over 18 years of age as culpable and exercising 'free choice', despite the evidence that the possibility of such a 'choice' has already been eroded.

Keeping these adult women in a quasi-criminal state through the laws on soliciting increases their vulnerability and contributes to their continued victimisation. Their propensity to report acts of violence, particularly by pimps or partners is circumscribed and the violence directed towards prostitutes by clients is no doubt motivated in part by assumptions about impunity. The continued criminalisation of street prostitutes seems therefore to inadvertently protect violent clients and pimps. It also, in general, sustains a position of dependence. Thus their passivity and lack of agency does not derive from seeing them as victims. On the contrary it arises predominately from their status as an offender. It is paradoxical that many of those who see women's involvement in prostitution as a result of 'free choice' also argue for the decriminalisation of prostitution. However, the conception that prostitution is an activity which is freely entered into, signals a woman's culpability and reaffirms her status as an offender rather than a victim.

We have seen that involvement in prostitution compounds and extends the range of victimisation which many of these women experience. There can be no other occupation that carries the same level of risk to health and personal well-being. Referring to prostitutes as victims does not imply an essentialism but rather recognises that their involvement in prostitution produces a range of different hazards which more or less directly affect their everyday lives and their future prospects. Denying 'victimhood' can lead to a denial of the disadvantaged and damaged nature of these women and tends to attribute a greater degree of agency and choice than women involved in prostitution are able to exercise.

We have seen the development of an array of services for young people involved in prostitution in recent years. A similar set of services and resources need to be put in place for those adult women involved in street prostitution. Victimisation and agency are not mutually exclusive. The women involved in prostitution express varying degrees of agency when deciding where and when to work, negotiating the conditions of their work and in the handling of clients. This however, does not mean that they do not at the same time experience systematic and widespread victimisation.

The other limitation to adult women involved in prostitution acquiring victim status comes from the fact that they are not, in many respects, 'ideal victims'. Because they are not generally seen as responsible or hard working, and enjoy a marginalised status, they are always going to be less than 'ideal' victims. Although those involved in prostitution are among the most severely victimised groups in society their status as victims remains uncertain. While the victim status of those under 18 has belatedly been recognised there remains a legacy of treating adult women as offenders rather than victims. This situation, in the UK at least, is changing and the policing of prostitution is turning, in principal and in practice, increasingly towards users and exploiters and away from the women. There is, however, a qualitative shift that still needs to occur in relation to those over the age of 18. The removal of the offence of 'soliciting for the purposes of prostitution' would be a necessary first step in making this conceptual transition.

Chapter 4

Pathways into prostitution

Introduction

A great deal has been written on how people become involved in prostitution. There are a large number of biographical and life history accounts that document in some detail the experiences of different women and girls (McConnell 2006; Roberts 2006). There is also a range of academic literature that has attempted to analyse processes and identify recurring themes. In fact, we now know a great deal about how predominantly young women become involved in prostitution in the UK and other countries, and much of the available research is mutually confirming (Hoigard and Finstad 1992; Melrose, Barrett and Brodie 1999; O'Neill 1997; Potter et al. 1999; Rickard 2001; Sharpe 1998; Weber et al. 2004).

The differences that arise centre around the different ways in which the available evidence is analysed, and the significance that is attributed to the different processes involved. The mode of interpretation and analyses of the research findings is, needless to say, critical in understanding the dynamics of entry, particularly if our aim is to develop appropriate preventative measures.

Thus, one of the surprising aspects of the literature on modes of entry into prostitution is the way in which some commentators claim that the complexity of the processes involved is such that they defy any straightforward or coherent explanation. Thus Marianne Hester and Nicole Westmarland (2004), in their overview of the processes by which people become involved in prostitution, state that: 'the evidence shows that young people become involved in prostitution through a series of complex and interrelated variables that are almost impossible to disentangle'. A recent NSPCC publication offering an overview of issues relating to young people involved in prostitution suggests that: 'Because young people involved in prostitution experience a multiple of interconnected problems it is often difficult to sort out the respective influence of these on an individual and impossible to identify any single cause. For this reason it is better to think of the factors involved as contributory problems' (Levy 2004: 31).

Thus in many of the studies which discuss entry into prostitution, causal relations are downplayed in favour of correlations which have limited explanatory value. As the above quotation suggests, a number of authors analyse the entry of women into prostitution in relation to a number of 'factors', which we are told interact or combine in such a way to propel individuals into prostitution. Other commentators distinguish between 'predisposing' and 'facilitating' factors or between 'background' and 'situational' factors in order to emphasise that not all factors have the same significance or role.

Alternatively, entry is seen as a combination of 'push' and 'pull' factors or in some accounts entry is seen as a consequence of 'drift'. All of these accounts in their own ways point to certain aspects of the ways in which individuals become involved in prostitution but fail to offer an explanation which is convincing, coherent or comprehensive. Before developing an alternative form of analysis some discussion of these various approaches is required. The multi-factor approach sees the involvement in prostitution as the outcome of a number of factors or variables, which like so many billiard balls collide in such a way that ultimately propels individuals into prostitution. In most of these accounts causal sequences are replaced by correlations, and it becomes difficult, if not impossible, to distinguish between necessary determinants and contingent events. In the process of dismissing the claim that there is a 'single' cause (which very few commentators actually argue) the issue of causality is dismissed entirely.

Closely related to the multi-factorial approach are those accounts that examine the process of entry into prostitution in terms of a series of risk factors. Risk analysis has become increasingly used in the social science literature in recent years and adds an apparent objectivity and scientificity to the more randomised and arbitrary multi-factorial approaches. For example, May and Hunter (2006), in their attempt to explain the role of drug use as a possible route into prostitution, deny the possibility of engaging in a causal analysis because they claim that:

> The causal relationship between problem drug use and involvement in sex work is hard to demonstrate in any precise way. However, drug use and street sex work largely share the same set of interconnecting risk factors, including disrupted family lines, socio-economic deprivation, child sexual abuse, experience of local authority care, homelessness, involvement in crime, disrupted schooling and low self-esteem.
>
> (May and Hunter 2006: 172)

The critical question of whether drug use precedes entry into prostitution is overshadowed by a form of risk analysis which groups and lists the factors seen to be related to entry into prostitution, but without weighting these factors, explaining the relation between them or examining how they may or may not combine. Risk analysis has been criticised for providing a thinly veiled subjectivism and as a strategy for obscuring the role and significance of key structural determinants in shaping outcomes (Silver and Miller 2002).

A variant of the multi-factor approach, which attempts to make a distinction between the impact of different factors and thereby overcome the apparent randomness of the analysis, is to see them as a combination of 'push' and 'pull' processes. Thus Margaret Melrose points out in her introduction to *Anchors in Floating Lives* that:

> All the contributors in this volume bear witness to the fact that young people become involved in commercial sexual exploitation for a range of complex and inter-connected – even overlapping – reasons and that it is seldom possible to pinpoint a single 'cause'. Rather there is a complex interaction between a range of 'push' and 'pull' factors and between individuals and environmental factors.
>
> (Melrose 2004: 7)

Similarly, Julia O'Connell Davidson (2000) claims that 'there is no simple or single answer to the question of how people become involved in prostitution'. Instead, she claims that existing international research:

> draws attention to a range of 'push' and 'pull' factors, including the use of force; deception or manipulation; poverty, hunger and economic need; social and political marginalisation; familial neglect and abuse; experience of sexual victimisation; peer influence; drug addiction; children's consumerism; children's desire for independence; excitement and or experience; children's sense of duty or responsibility for their kin.
>
> (O'Connell Davidson 2000: 46)

While this approach moves us towards a more differentiated form of analysis and captures a sense of the contradictory nature of the dynamics involved, it does not provide an adequate analytical framework for explaining the 'complex and interconnected' processes that are held to be in play.

Another way of grouping the various 'factors', which are seen to be associated with entry into prostitution, is to distinguish between 'predisposing' and 'precipitating' factors. The former are seen to be more fundamental and necessary factors while the latter set of factors are mobilised to explain why only a percentage of these exposed to the predisposing factors actually end up in prostitution (Silbert and Pines 1982; Benjamin and Masters 1964). In the various accounts that adopt this approach, however, there is little consistency in the identification of exactly what these 'predisposing' factors are. In some accounts it is economic factors or poverty. In others it is drug use, while some see psychological predisposition as the main predisposing factor. National and cultural differences may, of course, affect entry into prostitution but while these accounts are potentially useful in terms of identifying some of the main determinants they often seem to reflect the theoretical preoccupations of the researchers rather than the actual motivations of those entering prostitution.

A number of commentators have identified the process of entry into prostitution not so much in terms of the interaction of certain factors or of an identifiable decision-making process or a deliberate choice but rather as the consequences of a more uncertain and less conscious process of 'drift' (Davis 2000; Levy 2004; O'Neill 1997). Drawing on David Matza's (1964) classic examination of the ways in which people 'drift' into delinquency these authors explain that entry into prostitution as a result of 'temporarily removing the restraints that ordinarily control members of society'. Matza sees the process of drift being linked to the development of 'techniques of neutralisation' by which subjects are able to break or challenge conventional moralities and social norms. This approach focuses on the motivations of individuals and probes the conditions that will allow them to engage in prostitution, once the moral constraints have been loosened. Such conditions, Matza suggests, may involve desperation, excitement, or a mood of fatalism.

While providing an important antidote to those social control theories which deny volition and emphasising that entry into prostitution may be less deliberate or planned than is sometimes suggested, the focus on 'drift' tends to overlook or play down the structural processes that constrain the decision-making activities of individuals. The analysis tends to become too subjective or too vague. Thus all of these different types of explanation, while focusing on different aspects of entry into prostitution, are in different ways inadequate. On one side, they tend to import an unnecessary and disorientating level of complexity and uncertainty into the analysis. On another level, they appear vague and unfocused.

What is remarkable about the process of entry into prostitution is how similar the process is for many women and girls. In fact, it would seem that rather than entry being a product of a complex and impenetrable series of 'factors', that it may be better understood as a product of a number of identifiable 'stages' or 'pathways'. What is evident in reading the numerous available accounts of entry into prostitution is how many individuals appear to go through the same processes, have similar experiences, and are subject to the same determinants and constraints. Therefore, it would seem to be appropriate to draw upon the type of pathway analysis which various authors have used to good effect in analysing entry into crime and drug use (Parker et al. 1998; Sampson and Laub 1993).

If we examine the available academic and personal accounts (leaving aside the more sensational and voyeuristic variants) we see that for the vast majority of the women who currently work on the streets in Britain that there are remarkable similarities in their backgrounds and experiences. Although there are always some exceptions and not all women of course will take exactly the same route, it is possible to identify a series of stages and pathways through which the majority of the women involved in street prostitution move during the course of their lives.

Poverty and sexual ideology

It has been noted by many commentators that prostitution is at root 'economic' and that the main reason for entry is to earn money. This is no doubt, in essence, correct. However, it does not explain why many who are poor and deprived do not turn to prostitution in times of hardship. Nor does it explain why women choose to engage in prostitution rather than some other activity, legal or illegal, to earn money. More particularly, we need to explain why women stay in prostitution and how the motivation of a career or persistent prostitution differs from these women who sell sex on one or two occasions for whatever reason. There is a qualitative difference in the experience and identity of those who stay in prostitution for a period and who come to identify themselves as 'prostitutes' or 'working women' and those who may trade sex for money or goods on a few occasions (Katz 1991; McKegany and Barnard 1996).

Moreover, at the most general level, involvement in prostitution is structured by sexual ideologies whereby women are seen to 'supply' sex while men 'demand' it. This is often associated with myths about men's imperious sexual needs. Historically, the institutionalisation of prostitution has been mainly centred around female prostitutes servicing male clients. Thus, these structural conditions, dominant sexual ideologies and gender relations set the framework in which the decision to enter prostitution is made. There are, however, a number of more immediate processes that influence the decision to engage in prostitution. One of the most significant of these processes is child abuse and neglect.

Child abuse and neglect

Nearly all studies, which have examined the personal histories of street prostitutes, have focused on some form of abuse – either physical or sexual – or on forms of neglect within the household. Studies from around the world have repeatedly identified child abuse and neglect as providing a baseline experience, which affects a person's attitudes towards sex, towards themselves as well as towards others. The experience of different forms of neglect or abuse are widely seen as increasing the probability of an individual engaging in prostitution.

Estimates vary but studies from different countries suggest that between 50 to 90 per cent of those involved in street prostitution have histories of abuse and neglect. In one study carried out by May et al. (2001) in London, the researchers found that almost two thirds described their formative years as unhappy and half said that they had experienced some form of child abuse. In a retrospective study by Melrose et al. (1999) 21 out of 50 respondents reported that they had had their first sexual experience in the context of abuse. Pearce et al. (2002) found in their sample of 55 young people involved in prostitution that 25 had experienced sexual abuse in childhood. Similar findings have been found in numerous research studies on female prostitutes that have been carried out in America and Canada. In a classic study by Silbert and Pines (1982) it was reported that over 60 per cent of the women in their sample reported a history of physical abuse as children. In another study by Giobbe (1993) it was found that 90 per cent of the women had been physically battered in childhood, 74 per cent had been sexually abused by a family member, with a further 50 per cent also having been sexually abused by someone outside of their family (also see Bagley and Young 1987; Hunter 1994; Tyler et al. 2000).

The impact of family discord and neglect has also been noted in relation to young men involved in male homosexual prostitution:

> The impression left by this collection of personal histories is an over-whelming prevalence of disruption and discord in their early years. Gross physical neglect was less frequent than emotional deprivation. The majority had sprung form working class backgrounds where social problems were relatively frequent.
>
> (West 1992: 20)

Thus child sexual and physical abuse is not just a 'factor' which may or may not combine with other factors but provides a fundamental stage and set of experiences which make the decision to enter prostitution more probable. Farley and Kelly (2000) who have spent many years working with those who have been sexually abused point out that the experience of abuse and neglect in childhood can manifest itself in sexual and physical trauma. Traumatic re-enactments, they suggest, can occur 'alongside psychological dysfunctions, including self destructive thoughts and behaviours, self contempt, feelings of shame and worthlessness as well as sexual aversions and compulsions' (Farley and Kelly 2000: 42).

The experience of child abuse and neglect sets in motion a number of psychological and emotional responses that increase personal vulnerability. This is not only because they tend to affect the person's self esteem but also because as Julia Herman (1992) has explained they can have a number of other effects. These include the tendency to disassociate, and can create difficulties in establishing trust relationships. At the same time these childhood experiences encourage a need to prove loyalty and compliance as a condition for acceptance, self blaming and taking responsibility for the abuse, while developing a sense of 'inner badness' and self loathing. Although these processes are complex, and at times contradictory, their significance is that these childhood experiences are difficult to overcome and are likely to affect the well-being of these young people and their relations with others for much of their life.

The various experts have identified a number of the long term effects that sexual abuse and neglect can have on the propensity of young women to engage in prostitution. In cases where the abuse occurs in fragmented households, it may create family divisions and isolation or generate stigma from relatives and friends or alternatively result in a sense of secrecy and suspicion. It may disrupt education and the ability of individuals to concentrate and focus on schoolwork. Abuse may come to be seen as unavoidable or accepted as the inevitable price of relationships or as Herman (1992) has suggested: 'participation in forbidden sexual activity also confirms the child's sense of badness. Any gratification that a child is able to glean from the exploitative situation becomes proof that in her mind that she instigated and bears full responsibility for the abuse'.

Without wanting to over-pathologise those who engage in prostitution it does seem that child abuse or neglect is an important precursor for entry into prostitution and makes involvement in prostitution more likely at an early stage. In some respects entry into prostitution can be seen as a continuation and an adaption of the abuse experienced in childhood. A number of authors have pointed out that a difficult childhood is for many young women a first stage of entry into prostitution. Mansson and Hedin (1999), for example, in their study of 200 female prostitutes in Sweden found that almost 75 per cent had experienced a difficult childhood with 43 per cent being victims of sexual abuse. They note that:

> [However] our analysis shows that the way into the sex trade constitutes the culmination of a long chain of previous destructive events. We talk about a cycle of victimisation characterised by insufficient emotional connection, sexual abuse, sexual exploitation during teenage years, rape experiences and later on prostitution. . .Many of the women are labelled as 'whores', often long before their actual entry into prostitution. Given such a perspective, the women's debut into prostitution is often undramatic, even if the context in which it takes place can be quite chaotic.
>
> (Mansson and Hedin 1999: 71)

Since child abuse and neglect in the general population is relatively high, with the actual figure likely to be much higher than that which is reported, we need to be cautious about positing any direct link between child abuse and prostitution. It is almost certainly the case that those that have these experiences in childhood deal with them, deny them or overcome them. We also need to be sensitive to the differential impact of sexual and physical abuse as well as between sexual abuse and neglect. These experiences in childhood, however, appear to create some of the preconditions that make the decision to engage in prostitution more plausible. For the majority of those who eventually become involved in prostitution, however, these early life experiences need to be channelled in ways that make prostitution a more accessible and desirable option.

Running away and going into care

A further stage of progression involves the process of running away or entering the 'care' of local authorities. Again much of the available literature has pointed out the importance of both these routes in the decision to enter prostitution. Both are closely associated with what are described in official circles as 'dysfunctional families', child abuse and neglect, and it is a reasonable assumption that those who run away from home or who are placed in the care of local authorities tend to be those who are most systematically abused or neglected or who come from broken homes.

It has been estimated that one in three women involved in street prostitution have been in local authority care (O'Neill 1997; Cusick et al. 2003). These 'care' institutions, it would seem, rather than providing the necessary care and support to turn the lives of these neglected or abused children around, all too often become sites for involvement in crime in general and prostitution in particular. This experience is not however limited to the UK as Hoigard and Finstad (1992) note in the research on prostitution in Norway. Fifteen of the 26 women they interviewed had been institutionalised before they had turned their first 'trick'. They emphasised that:

> This is an important discovery – not only because these figures tell of young women who are already neglected by normal society before they become prostitutes but also because institutions are revealed to be important training grounds for prostitution. In institutions many young people in trouble are stored together like surplus wreckage. They often run away together without money. What could be more natural than they exchange knowledge about ways to survive?
>
> (Hoigard and Finstad 1992: 16)

The experience of marginalisation and institutionalisation, it is suggested, creates both the social distance and the contacts which may lead those that are susceptible into prostitution. Institutionalisation can also take the form of imprisonment and this experience often serves to further marginalise and stigmatise those concerned.

For those who run away from local authority care or from home it is estimated that most will resort to crime and/or prostitution in order to survive within six weeks (Kirby 1995; Green et al. 1997). It has been estimated by the Social Exclusion Unit in 2001 that by the age of 16 some 77,000 young people in the UK ran away from home, normally a result of 'family problems'. At the same time, they note, there is a severe lack of accommodation and facilities for those who run away. In England, for example, there is only one refuge for children under 16, which is based in London. It has eight beds and provides accommodation for up to two weeks. The Social Exclusion Unit report points out that there is no national policy on runaways, and that few receive any significant help in addressing the problems that they ran away from. They also note that there is a circular relation between running away and going into care with runaways being more likely to be sent into care, while those in care frequently run away. Running away from home is also seen to increase the likelihood of becoming homeless later in life. Family problems are reported to be the cause of running away from home for 80 per cent of young people and those that run away are predominantly from poor and deprived backgrounds. The Social Exclusion Unit report notes that the closure of three of the four 'safe houses' in the UK has left young runaways with few options and they call for the development of a set of clear policies about how local agencies should respond to this issue.

Homelessness or living in temporary or insecure accommodation has been found to be prevalent among women involved in prostitution. May et al. (2001) found that three-quarters of women working in the Kings Cross area of London were either homeless or living in temporary accommodation. Campbell (2002) found that nearly two thirds of the 70 women she interviewed in Liverpool were of no fixed abode and Phoenix (1999) reported that 18 of 21 women that she interviewed had recurring housing problems.

American research reveals similar links between running away from home and involvement in prostitution. The number of young people who are estimated to runaway is as many as two million annually. The connection between running away and involvement in prostitution, it has been suggested, is a function of how long children run away and their motivation for doing so. Thus the critical questions in terms of runaways and the likelihood of becoming involved in prostitution are; how long they stay away, how far they travel, how often do they runaway and how old are they? Barri Flowers (2001) makes a distinction between runaways who leave home and 'throwaways' who are thrown out of home. Although the proportion of 'throwaways' is considerably less than runaways a greater percentage of 'throwaways' are young girls.

It is estimated that as many as one million teenage runaways become involved in some form of prostitution in America annually. Leaving home for any period increases vulnerability and victimisation. According to the National Centre for Missing and Exploited Children (1999) up to 77 per cent of prostitution in the US involves teenagers running away from home. Around 30 per cent of runaway prostitutes were found to be street kids living in shelters. Runaways need food, shelter and often seek companionship. Thus they are easy prey for pimps and procurers. It is reported that up to 90 per cent of young girls involved in prostitution either began under the direction of a pimp, or became involved with one in the course of their involvement in prostitution (Flowers 2001).

Peers, pimps and procurers

No matter how desperate for money a person might be, it is a very daunting prospect to stand on the streets, find a male client and negotiate the provision of sexual services – particularly if the person is young has low self-esteem and generally feels vulnerable. Engaging in these activities normally requires some element of facilitation either by peers, pimps or procurers (Nadon et al. 1998).

Estimates of the proportion of women entering prostitution who have been influenced by pimps or procurers vary considerably by age and location. Research suggests, however, that young women are more likely to be pimped than older women. A study by Barnardo's found that the majority of the young women aged between 12 and 14 that they interviewed did not make their own decision to sell sexual services but were groomed and then coerced by men aged 18–25 (Swann 1998). This process of grooming has, according to Swann, a number of key elements involving enslaving, creating dependencies, taking control and finally total dominance. This grooming process requires skilled manipulation and control on the part of the pimp.

It has been noted that pimps and procurers target young people in care seeing them as vulnerable and accessible. It has also been reported that pimps procure women by encouraging them to become addicted to drugs, particularly crack cocaine, and then using the drug dependency as a way of motivating women to become involved in prostitution (Faugier and Sargeant 1997). The shift to drug-related pimping has been noted by a number of researchers but it has also been reported that these relationships frequently involve coercion. In the study by May et al. (2000), for example, six out of 19 women attributed their involvement in prostitution directly to coercive pimps. In some cases the women had to fund their own drug use and that of their pimp/partner. All 19 women had experienced physical abuse from their pimps ranging from 'slaps' to hospitalisation. Ten women said they had been raped by their pimps or otherwise sexually abused.

American research suggests that although there may have been an increase in 'independent' prostitution in some areas that over half of those entering prostitution do so with a pimp (Giobbe 1993). The involvement with a pimp is seen to perpetuate women in 'the game' since the pimp will do what he can to maintain the women's involvement in prostitution (Williamson and Cluse-Tolar 2002). The aim of the pimp is to exploit the vulnerabilities and aspirations of these women, while the would-be prostitute is often looking for affection, protection and direction.

Belatedly, policy makers have begun to respond to this situation and have introduced legislation to try to prevent vulnerable young women being introduced into prostitution by pimps and procurers. In England and Wales in 2003, legislation in the form of the Sexual Offences Act has addressed the issue of 'sexual grooming' in which adults who meet or communicate with children under 16 with the intent of engaging them in sexual activity are to be subject to more severe penalties. As with all such legislation there is a problem of gaining evidence and showing intent, but this piece of legislation at least signals a growing official commitment to protect children from sexual abuse (Ost 2004). The same piece of legislation made it an offence 'for any person who cares or incites another person to become a prostitute for gain, or who controls any of the activities of a prostitute'. This aspect of the legislation broadens the focus beyond the traditional image of the 'pimp' and includes 'any person'.

The other major facilitating process is the introduction into prostitution by peers. Margaret Melrose (1999), for example, found that half of the young women in her sample became involved in prostitution through peer group association. The introduction into prostitution by peers appears to be particularly pronounced among the homeless and those in care. Melrose argues that peer group relations and contacts may be equally, if not more, important in encouraging entry into prostitution than pimps and procurers. Canadian research has come to similar conclusions and found that a large number of respondents were introduced to prostitution by female friends, or institutional room-mates or by family members who were already involved in prostitution (Busby et al. 2002).

Routes and pathways into prostitution

An examination of the available research suggests that there are considerable similarities, even in different countries, about the routes into prostitution. It is therefore possible to construct a three stage model in which stage one involves 'predisposition' of young people through abuse and neglect in 'dysfunctional families'. The second stage involves the processes of marginalisation and stigmatisation, which can compound the vulnerabilities established in stage one or alternatively generate new pathways. Stage three involves 'facilitation' and introduction of individuals into prostitution either by pimps and procurers or by peers and associates. Not all women will pass through all three stages but a considerable percentage will pass through at least two of these stages and normally in the sequence outlined.

The implications of this form of analysis is that it allows us to map out pathways into prostitution and begins to identify the main processes involved in a way that is both causal and sequential rather than seeing entry into prostitution as result of a series of contingent factors. Pathways analysis also provides the possibility of overcoming the problem of structure and agency. It recognises that people make choices but within certain structures and constraints (see Figure 4.1 below).

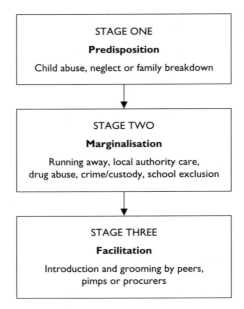

Figure 4.1 Routes into prostitution.

In a study carried out by Barnardo's, they present the case of Emma. This case is depressingly typical of many of the young women who become involved in street prostitution and provides an example of someone who goes along the pathways suggested in the above analysis. She was:

> Sexually abused by her mother's boyfriend and starved of any love and attention at home. Emma met her older boyfriend Roger when she was 12 and soon began running away from home. 'I just needed someone to tell me nice things like how beautiful I was.' says Emma. 'I'd never been told that before, ever. I just needed attention really badly.' 'He was so abusive and had a drug problem. He probably spotted me as an easy target and because I was so desperate for love I decided to stick with it.' Before long, Roger and Emma got involved in alcohol and pressured her into having sex with other men. The money paid for his drugs. Emma ended up staying at a crack house. She tried to leave but Roger threatened her and stalked her.
>
> (Palmer and Stacey 2002: 7)

There is no shortage of similar stories in the literature on prostitution. The case of Emma, like so many others, embodies the recurring themes of neglect, the search for attention, running away and social marginalisation, the preda-tory role of the pimp in facilitating entry into prostitution and then using threats to prevent the person from leaving. Significantly, Barnardo's no longer talk about 'child prostitutes, pimps and punters' but more realistically describe participants as 'children abused through prostitution', 'abusing adults' and 'child sex offenders'.

Age of entry into prostitution

In recent years, there has been a growing recognition that a significant percentage of those involved in prostitution first became involved at a very young age. One study by the Children's Society, which examined the experiences of young people who had become involved in prostitution, reported that out of 50 young adults the majority started before they were 18 years old. Over half had started by the age of 14 and two were only 11 years of age when they first engaged in prostitution. Predictably, most of the children came from a background of family discord, poverty, abuse and violence, which led to them feeling violated, unloved and neglected. Over half were runaways, mainly from local authority care homes (Melrose, Barrett and Brodie 1998).

Other research by May et al. (1999) found that half of those interviewed became involved in prostitution while they were still minors. Hester and Westmarland (2004) in a review of a number of Home Office-funded research studies found that 64 per cent of women first became involved in prostitution under the age of eighteen. Hoigard and Finstad (1992) found in their Norwegian study that the average age for the women's first 'trick' was 15½.

Research conducted by the Department of Health in 2002 found that there were over 600 children involved in prostitution in England (Swann and Balding 2002). In this report it was suggested that the priority should be to provide care, guidance and support for those less than 18 years of age who are involved in prostitution or at risk of becoming involved. They advocate a multi-agency approach and argue that the primary law enforcement effort should be directed at 'abusers and coercers'. However, it is apparent that the activities of the police and Social Services are largely reactive rather than proactive and that the Area Child Protection Committees (ACPCs) who are charged with investigating and prosecuting those who coerce and abuse children through prostitution are relatively ineffective.

The Department of Health report found that while three out of four APCS had some specialist police resources for tackling prostitution, in the remaining 25 per cent either specialist police intervention was not available or respondents did not know about the availability of police resources for tackling this issue. Responses to the survey also show that police activity was largely reactive with only 56 per cent gathering intelligence on both abusers and coercers. Only 10 per cent of the ACPCs had successfully prosecuted coercers and abusers, although four reported that 78 young people had been identified as being involved in prostitution but that no perpetrators had been convicted. There were reports of considerable delays in bringing cases to court, gathering and mobilising evidence, and it was reported that in some areas the police would not act unless they were sure that a prosecution was probable. In sum, the report indicates that responses are patchy and not particularly well coordinated, with a lack of good quality data and a limited availability of specialist resources in many areas.

Swann and Balding (2002) note that only three out of 50 ACPCs report that they were achieving their aims of prosecuting abusers/coercers. One of these ACPCs was Nottingham, which reported 60 successful prosecutions for offences against children. This reflects the potential scale of child prostitution nationally and at the same time serves as a serious indictment of those ACPCs in different parts of the country who still allow abusers to go unchecked and unpunished.

Drug use and entry into prostitution

A great deal has been written on drug use as a route into prostitution. Involvement in heavy drug use is seen as significant in this respect because it increases the vulnerability and marginalisation of women and also their need for a considerable amount of quick cash. At the same time the drug use can moderate the tensions, pressures and difficulties of engaging in prostitution. There is a danger, however, of giving too much priority to drug use as an independent process and to overlook its links with the personal histories and lifestyles of those involved in prostitution.

The central role accorded to drug use is largely a function of snapshot surveys of street prostitutes that indicate that in the UK between 50 to 90 per cent are problematic drug users addicted to heroin or crack cocaine or both (Hester and Westmarland 2004). Just as in the debate about crime the common wisdom is that drug use leads to crime because people need money to support their habit, so a similar logic is often used to 'explain' the link between drug use and prostitution. However, these types of explanation are too simplistic and exclude the complex links between drug use and other processes which increase the likelihood of people becoming involved in prostitution.

The evidence that there is a much lower level of drug addiction among those who work in brothels suggests that the role of drugs in propelling women into prostitution in general may be less than is often claimed (Weitzer 2000; Sanders 2005). Various studies have shown that while a considerable percentage of those who end up working on the streets have been involved in some form of drug use from an early age, many of these studies do not distinguish clearly between experimental, recreational, habitual and problematic drug use (see Parker et al. 1998). Therefore, it is often difficult to identify the nature and intensity of drug use amongst those involved in prostitution before they became prostitutes. Most of the critical questions about the patterns and history of drug use are rarely addressed in the literature and therefore the role of drugs in propelling women into prostitution is not fully examined with the consequence that the effect of drug use on involvement in prostitution remains unclear, despite the emphasis placed on drug use as a major 'factor' leading women into prostitution. The uncertainty arises from the fact that many of the studies ask respondents whether they have *ever* used certain drugs before entry into prostitution and often fail to make any clear distinction between controlled or problematic drug use. Thus what is missing from much of the research is an analysis of the developments of drug use over time, the frequency and quantities used and its meaning for the user.

Many people sustain heavy drug use over a period without engaging in prostitution (Melrose 2007). The significance of many drug users may be as much to do with the marginalised status and the lifestyle, as it has to do with the level of consumption. Other researchers have suggested that once women become involved in prostitution that their drug use is likely to increase in order to make the work more bearable. McKeganey and Barnard (1996) noted in their study in Glasgow that drug-injecting prostitutes often report an escalation of their drug consumption after becoming involved in prostitution.

One large-scale American study which employed a form of pathways analysis found in a sample of 1,142 female jail detainees found that drug use was less significant than is normally expected. They found that:

> Running away had a dramatic effect on entry into prostitution in early adolescence but little effect later in the life course. Childhood sexual victimisation, by contrast, nearly doubled the odds of entry into prostitution throughout the lives of women. Although the prevalence of drug use was significantly higher among prostitutes than non-prostitutes, drug abuse did not explain entry into prostitution.
>
> (McClanahan et al. 1999: 1606)

While this study accepts that drug use may play a role in the process of entry, the authors note that there is a disproportionate level of drug use amongst abused children and runaways and therefore the precise role of drug use is often difficult to untangle. The implication of these findings is that a significant number of women may have become involved in prostitution irrespective of their use of illicit drugs (Potterat et al. 1998). Some researchers have questioned whether drug use is a cause of entry or whether it is better seen as a symptom of a range of socio-economic and personal issues. The implication being that if it is more of a symptom than a generic cause that its removal or reduction may have limited effect on the deep-seated reasons why women become involved in prostitution (Buchanan 2004).

Trapping and remaining in prostitution

In an informative study on identity formation amongst those involved in prostitution conducted by Joanna Phoenix (1999) she notes that many of the young women who become involved in prostitution do so in order to gain independence and financial rewards. However, she explains that once involved they often experience various forms of dependency and limited financial stability. Indeed, their involvement in prostitution often tends to compound rather than resolve their problems. Thus:

> The social material and ideological conditions that circumscribed the interviewees earlier lives by structuring their poverty, their community and social ostracism and their dependence on men or state welfare benefits led them to see prostitution as a way forward and a realistic (and successful) strategy for achieving independence, financial and housing security and new social networks. But there was a paradox in the interviewee's narratives. For at the same time as describing it as a means to achieve economic and social stability, they also described it as a 'trap' that further circumscribed their lives and brought even greater poverty, community ostracism, exploitation, abuse, housing difficulties, dependence on men, and thus threatened their social, material and at times physical survival.
>
> (Phoenix 1999: 100)

Thus in her study Phoenix found that the independence and security which young women seek when entering prostitution proves to be illusory and that instead they often experience new forms of dependency and insecurity. The critical concept in this process is 'trapping' which suggests that once women are involved in prostitution many find themselves entangled in a whole series of dependencies that draw them in and makes the possibility of leaving prostitution more difficult. It is this process which aims to explain the length of time that women will remain in prostitution and in some cases why women end up by being involved in prostitution for considerably longer than they intended.

Linda Cusick and Matthew Hickman (2005) have developed the notion of 'trapping' to examine the relationship between different vulnerabilities and involvement in prostitution and drug use. Their approach involves making predictions about the likelihood of 'trapping' as a function of previous experiences. Thus they state that:

> Three quarters of participants had used drugs and had sold sex before the age of 18. Half had been in care and half had been homeless. One in five (21%) had run away or left home before 16 and 50% had been convicted for acquisitive offences. Nevertheless, these experiences did not explain 'trapping'. There were strong associations between being trapped and outdoor/drift sex work (92%). After adjustment for the other vulnerabilities in the logistic regression only outdoor/drift sex work remained significant; with sex workers involved in outdoor/drift sex

work having an adjusted odds ratio of over 7 (95% c.i.1.7 to 28.3) of being trapped.

(Cusick and Hickman 2005: xx)

This Home Office-funded research however, is based on a very selective sample of women drawn predominantly from those already involved in voluntary and statutory agencies rather than a more representative sample of women working on the street. The potentially important finding of this research is that just over half of the participants reported starting 'hard' drugs use before they became involved in prostitution, while just over 20 per cent reported starting 'hard drug use' after they became involved in prostitution, with a further 23 per cent reporting starting hard drug use in the same year as starting, is obscured in this analysis. Thus it suggests that for only half of the women in this sample, hard drug use preceded their involvement in prostitution (see Cusick, Martin and May 2003).

However, the finding in this survey that 59 per cent are currently problematic drug users and 41 per cent reported having a drug problem 'in the past' is too vague and does not to allow us to identify how the involvement in prostitution affects the use of drugs and particularly problematic drug use. It is also not clear whether the 59 per cent who are currently problematic drug users are comprised of the same population who were 'hard' drug users before engaging in prostitution. Thus on the central issue of how drug use affects 'trapping' the research is unable to provide an answer. For those who have engaged in drug treatment programmes we do not know what kind of drugs people have stopped using or why, except that we are told that the most effective forms of drug treatment programmes were found to be residential.

The term 'trapped' in this context has a very specific meaning and it was noted that participants are deemed to be 'trapped' if they had ongoing problematic drug use and were continuing to sell sex at the time of the interview. The research attempted to test the hypotheses that background vulnerabilities are most reinforcing when they are concentrated. In fact, however, the research is not able to really test this hypothesis at all since the sample is skewed, we are not given information on the quantities or the types of drug used over time, or the role of coercion or other structural pressures that might reinforce women's involvement in prostitution. The interesting questions which the research raises are therefore not effectively addressed and future research is needed which involves a more representative sample and adopts a different methodological approach.

Conclusion

As we have seen there is a considerable level of consensus about how people become involved in prostitution. We know that the vast majority of women who become involved in prostitution are poor and disadvantaged.

However, it is only a percentage of the poor who decide on this option. To explain the process by which a certain percentage of poor people become involved in prostitution it has been suggested that multi-factor, push-pull accounts, and seeing entry into prostitution as a form of 'drift' capture certain elements of the process but do not provide an adequate account of the routes and stages which the majority of women engaged in street prostitution go through. In response, it has been suggested that a form of 'pathways' analysis based on an examination of the 'life course' of individuals and groups provides a potentially better way of understanding entry and involvement in prostitution.

The use of pathways analysis and the identification of different routes and stages, allows the formulation of a differentiated and structured approach to prevention. It suggests that interventions can be targeted at each of these three stages and that effective measures can be put in place to prevent, deter and redirect those 'at risk' of engaging in prostitution. It also moves us beyond randomised and contingent accounts and provides the basis for the development of a more coordinated set of policies and practices. It also indicates the need for a new type of research agenda that can examine the role of different routes and pathways in relation to involving and sustaining women in prostitution.

Having become involved in prostitution the subsequent issue is what processes reinforce the involvement of women or 'trap' them into prostitution. The research by Cusick and Hickman (2003) is correct to raise the issue but unfortunately does not provide a form of analysis that is able to throw much light on the processes involved. In particular, in relation to drug use we are provided with little useful information on attitudes towards drugs once women become involved in prostitution. The process of 'trapping', however, requires further exploration because previous research has indicated that not only is there a tendency for drug use to increase significantly during the period of involvement in prostitution, but that there are other processes at work which reinforce a woman's involvement in prostitution and may militate against her desire to exit.

Chapter 5

Desistance and exiting from prostitution

Introduction

Many people think of prostitution as a 'career' or even a 'profession', but for most of those who become involved in prostitution the intention is often to be involved for a limited period of time. Research carried out in London, for example, in the mid 1980s found that the majority of women involved in street prostitution worked on a short term or sporadic basis, normally to meet pressing financial needs. The second largest group involved mainly women who had come to London for an anticipated two or three year period to make some money in order to make their lives more financially stable. Many of these 'away day' women, however, remained involved in prostitution for five or six years. The third group involved what might be referred to as the 'career' women. This group involved less than 10 per cent of the total (Matthews 1986a). Similar typologies have been developed by American researchers. Potterat et al. (1998) have divided women involved in prostitution into 'evanescent' workers who engage a few days or weeks annually, 'short-term' workers who work intermittently for weeks or even months, and 'long term' workers who work for a number of years.

Although the composition of street prostitution in London and other parts of the UK has changed significantly over the last two decades, these studies remind us that different women have a differential involvement in prostitution and that there is a regular 'turnover' of those involved in prostitution without any formal outside intervention. Thus, it is necessary when examining the processes by which women leave prostitution to distinguish between the effects of personal and informal decision-making processes and more formal interventions instigated by the relevant agencies, otherwise we may overestimate the effectiveness of formal interventions. For the sake of clarity, we will refer to the informal decision-making process as 'desistance', while leaving prostitution primarily as a result of formal interventions will be referred to as 'exiting'. Since both desistance and exiting are processes rather than events, and the decision to leave prostitution often involves a combination of informal and formal pressures it will not always be easy to differentiate between them. However, the methodological challenge in evaluating the effectiveness of exiting programmes is to determine their added value and the relation between informal decision-making and the impact of different formal interventions.

In examining the process of desistance and exiting the aim is to develop the pathways analysis outlined above and to identify the relations between routes into and routes out of prostitution, as well as the turning points, 'traps' or 'snares' which may prolong involvement in prostitution. It is important to note, however, that even amongst those who have been involved in prostitution for a number of years this involvement may not have been continuous. For example, one study of young people involved in prostitution found that:

> Half the sample (25) had been continuously involved in prostitution since they had first become involved. Among the other half of the sample people had occasionally taken breaks and sometimes for a couple of months, sometimes to take up 'formal' employment and sometimes as a result of having been in prison.
>
> (Melrose 1999: 39)

Routes out of prostitution

In Sampson and Laub's (1993) examination of pathways they point out that desistance is not simply the reversal of the processes that lead people into particular activities, but will often be a function of other processes including maturation, negative experiences, developing new relationships or changing location. Their research indicates that childhood experiences do not necessarily determine desistance, although they may influence it (Sampson and Laub 2003; 2003a). A similar point is also made by David Farrington (1992) who suggests that it is social influences from peers and spouses and significant others that are most likely to affect desistance.

Since we rarely know whether the non-involvement in prostitution is a temporary or permanent situation desistance is not necessarily termination but needs to be defined as the 'sustained absence from a particular event' (Maruna 2000). Leaving prostitution may be a slow procedural process with continuous reversals and deviations. Rarely does it take the form of a quick and clean break.

One of the central issues in pathways analysis is whether particular routes of entry are associated with the length of stay in prostitution and the difficulties leaving. A central hypothesis is that the earlier the age of involvement the longer the career. Moffitt (1994) for example argues that, in general, it is a function of the onset of the anti-social behaviour, mastery of conventional pro-social skills, and the severity of the 'snares' or 'traps' encountered. Amongst 'snares' and 'traps', Moffitt includes imprisonment and other sanctions which further marginalise, stigmatise or increase the dependencies of individuals.

For women who want to leave prostitution there are a number of obstacles that have to be overcome. Women involved in street prostitution will in many cases have a police record for prostitution and drug-related offences, and consequently, find it difficult to secure alternative forms of employment. Moreover, the high level of drug dependency among this group makes the possibility of operating in the legitimate labour market slim. Many will have low educational levels and few skills and qualifications. For others there may be unresolved psychological problems caused by a history of abuse. Further, after a period of involvement in prostitution many of these women will have difficulties in forming and sustaining normal relationships and have difficulty in trusting others, particularly men. For some it is the money and the difficulty of earning similar amounts in other ways. For others it is the growing familiarity with the lifestyle and the flexibility of the working arrangements that may be hard to give up. Hoigard and Finstad (1992) suggest that the problems of leaving prostitution are bound up with feelings of shame, problems of identity, feelings of insecurity and overcoming marginalisation and stigmatisation. In some cases, women are pressured or forced to remain in prostitution although they would like to give it up (Boynton 1998: 64). In situations in which the prostitute has a drug-dependent partner whose habit she is financing there can be considerable pressure to continue working, although she may want to leave prostitution.

The main factors which appear to be influential in the decision to leave prostitution are age, experience of serious violence, meeting a new partner, changing locations, losing their children and reducing drug dependency. Desistance, however, often occurs in phases with interruptions and reversals. Thus, the period of desistance may last months, and in some cases, years. The decision to desist from prostitution is in many ways more difficult than the decision to enter prostitution. In fact, the decision to give up prostitution may be the first time that the women involved in prostitution make a deliberate and positive choice about the direction of their lives. It is often a tough choice that requires considerable determination and commitment.

Explaining desistance

Just as becoming a prostitute involves a process of identity formation and is not just an 'event' involving the exchange of sexual services for money or reward, so leaving prostitution often involves a change of identity and a redefinition of self. The work of Shadd Maruna (2000) in relation to the rehabilitation of offenders is instructive in this respect. Maruna argues that overcoming a history of deviant behaviour and coming to see oneself as a non-deviant person is a key to personal change. Those who are able to sustain a non-essentialist view of themselves are more likely to be able to change.

Similarly, those who manage to maintain a distinction between their involvement in prostitution and their private lives are more likely to be able to leave when they choose to.

The important point which Maruna (2000) makes is that women who want to leave prostitution need to develop a coherent account of how their new identity departs from, but simultaneously accounts for, their past. Thus the aim is not to negate or deny the past but see the past as a necessary stepping stone towards the future. By coming to terms with their past they are able to explain to themselves (and others) why they are not like that anymore. Thus the new identity is seen simultaneously as a continuation and a rupture with the past. It is important, Maruna argues, to move beyond fatalism and self-remorse and to see the past for what it is – the past. The aim is not to negate the past, instigate repentance, shame or recriminations but to put the past to use to serve as a reference point to help guide the individual and others in the desired direction.

Burnett and Maruna (2004) suggest that the concept of 'hope' is significant in this process. Although it may appear at first a 'fuzzy' concept, they use the term to mean 'an individual's overall perception that personal goals can be achieved'. This involves the identification of available pathways to achieving desired goals. Having 'hope' therefore involves having both the 'will' and the 'way' to achieve change. Those who maintain their involvement in anti-social behaviour, Burnett and Maruna argue, have a general fatalistic mindset and feel that their destiny is not of their control, although they recognise that these decisions are always subject to external constraints.

Pathways analysis is a useful approach in this respect since it aims to move beyond the structure-agency dichotomy. It allows for agency but recognises that decisions will take place within structures and be conditioned by external processes. It also distinguishes individual from social processes and is thereby able to move beyond the voluntarism associated with the 'free choice' perspective. Thus it is recognised that change involves the provision of opportunities and the willingness of individuals to take these opportunities (France and Homel 2006).

Mansson and Hedin (1999) have developed a model of desistance in relation to the interplay of individual and social processes. The most important elements they suggest are childhood experiences, financial pressures, survival strategies, and interplay with male customers. They have developed a model of desistance from prostitution based on notions of status transition and role exit which involves three consecutive phases (i) first doubts involving a questioning of the role, (ii) seeking alternatives, (iii) reaching a turning point in the creation of the new role.

The 'turning point' is seen as critical and it is suggested that a traumatic incident or a positive life event can generate a point of change or transition. The main reasons that women gave in Mansson and Hedin's research for deciding to leave prostitution were wanting to regain the custody of their children, being pregnant, or that they had been befriended (in some cases by clients) and given help and support; or alternatively that they have experienced a violent or traumatic event or simply they felt that they were too old.

Teela Sanders (2007) has examined the different motivations for leaving prostitution among those women who work on the street and those who work indoors. She suggests that while street workers often decide to leave prostitution as a result of violent incidents, ill health, loss of children, or imprisonment and tend to move through a planned drug treatment programme, re-housing and therapeutic engagement, the women who work off-street tend to leave because they enter new relationships, develop an alternative career, become disillusioned with working conditions or simply feel that they have been involved in prostitution long enough and that it is time for a change. The implications are that those working off street tend to be mainly desisters and leave prostitution largely as a result of their own volition, while those working on the street normally 'exit' with the help of a range of different support agencies.

Harm reduction and beyond

The damaged, disorganised and dependent nature of many of the women who currently work on the streets in Britain and elsewhere, together with the various pressures which maintain women in prostitution, mean that the majority of the women who work on the street and who want to leave prostitution require some form of external support. Increasingly, a growing proportion of the agencies which have been set up to support women involved in prostitution over the last decade in the UK are incorporating 'exiting' strategies into their remit. In some areas continued funding requires that agencies sign up to the provision of an exiting programme.

As women involved in prostitution become seen more as victims rather than offenders, there has been an increasing emphasis on providing different forms of support for those who want to leave prostitution. A range of interventions have been developed over the last decade or so to improve sexual health, reduce drug dependency, limit violence against working women and respond to their housing and other needs. There has been a growth in outreach work, one-to-one support and the provision of drop-in centres as well as in the referral of clients to specialist services (Bindel 2006).

The vast majority of support agencies operate with a harm reduction model of intervention and there can be no doubt that this approach has resulted in an improvement of the formerly ignored health problems of marginalised populations. The harm reduction model tends to take a non-judgemental approach and maintain that the individuals' decision to enter prostitution should be respected, and that the role of intervention is to reduce some of the negative consequences of involvement in prostitution. Developed mainly in relation to HIV/AIDS in the mid 1980s the harm reduction or harm minimisation approach has subsequently been mainstreamed and is a major strategy for dealing with a range of social problems including drug addiction and prostitution (McKeganey 2006).

There are, however, three critical questions that arise in relation to the development of harm reduction approaches directed towards prostitution. The first is what are the most serious harms which need to be addressed? Second, what are the most appropriate or effective measures that can be mobilised to reduce these harms? Third, to what extent does reducing the harms associated with prostitution impact on the experience of other groups?

A response to the first question involves the identification of the most serious harms associated with prostitution. Currently, these are identified by most of the groups that have been set up to support prostitutes as sexual health, drug addiction and violence from male clients. Addressing these harms aims to promote a safer and healthier working environment for women involved in prostitution, rather than encouraging them to leave prostitution. Indicatively, the violence perpetrated by pimps and partners is not normally addressed in this harm reduction approach. In some areas, housing needs are considered, but it is less common to deal with the psychological or emotional needs of women. The harm minimisation approach, however, tends to obscure discussion over values and priorities. In particular, the things to be considered as harms to be reduced largely become practical, technical or medical matters. The issue of what is an acceptable level of harm or what is an adequate level of reduction is rarely specified (Miller 2001; O'Malley 2006).

The second issue concerns the development of appropriate strategies to reduce identified harms. For the most part the main harm reduction policies which have emerged in relation to violence have involved the development of 'ugly mugs' and 'dodgy punters' campaigns, placing pressure on the police to investigate reported incidents and to encourage women to work in designated areas and to look out for each other. Although these various strategies may have some effect, their overall impact on reducing violence against women involved in prostitution appears to be limited. This is mainly because even when violent clients are known to be in the area a considerable percentage of the women carry on working as was recently demonstrated by events in Ipswich. For those who are heavily drug addicted the ability to take precautions or to identify potentially dangerous clients may be limited. Moreover, most of the serious incidents occur not at the point at which women are picked up but in remote spots where it is difficult or impossible to police or seek assistance. Where serious assaults against prostitutes are reported in the UK they are taken more seriously by the police than they were 10 years ago. However, the continued high level of serious violence directed towards women involved in prostitution suggests that the harm minimisation approach in this respect has been of limited effectiveness.

Similar arguments could be mobilised in relation to forms of drug treatment directed towards women involved in prostitution. Despite the fact that addressing problematic drug use has been a priority in many areas the reported levels of drug use remain consistently high amongst this group. This may, of course, not only be to do with the relative ineffectiveness of drug treatment programmes and more to do with the pressures to increase levels of drug consumption among working women in order to be able to cope with the strains and tensions of the work. The issue that arises is whether the aim is to 'patch up' those with drug and other problems enough so that they can continue working on the street or whether the aim is to provide a form of 'root and branch' intervention aimed at addressing problematic drug use, even if this means encouraging women to stop working on the streets.

Much of the discussion in relation to harm reduction is pitched at the individual level rather than at collectivity and tends to concentrate on addressing the harms experienced by certain women rather than the harm caused by prostitution to other social groups. Reference has already been made to the ways in which street prostitution can impact upon the quality of life of local residents, particularly women. Apart from local residents the families and children of those involved in prostitution may experience shame, stress and anxiety. It may be the case that some women engage in prostitution to support their children but because of the lifestyle and the tendency towards problematic drug use, children may be neglected and taken into care which itself can be a route for recruiting the next generation of those who engage in prostitution.

It has also been suggested that the harm reduction approach inadvertently supports abusers of exploiters. By providing condoms, lubricants, health checks, limiting violence from clients and the like, while generally turning a blind eye to issues of coercion and exploitation, the various interventions which are associated with harm reduction serve to increase earnings and allow women to work for longer, although in many cases the women concerned are only able to keep a fraction of the money that they earn.

There are other related developments that have called into question the utility of the harm reduction approach in relation to the growing interest in developing exiting strategies. Despite the huge amounts of time and money, which has been spent on ostensibly reducing harms, the population of street prostitutes appears to be more damaged, drug addicted and disorganised than ever. The main effect of these interventions, it would appear, has been to sustain them in prostitution for longer than they otherwise might have done. It is also the case that there is little incentive to promote exiting strategies, since if effective it would remove the need for the support agencies themselves. But as the women working on the streets of Britain are visibly more disorganised and drug addicted, it is becoming evident that assisting them to leave prostitution requires a more committed and proactive response which is able to provide active encouragement, rather than waiting for women to request help to leave prostitution.

It should be noted that the harm minimisation approach adopted by most of the support agencies occurs against a background of illegality and enforcement. These options represent the familiar tension in the policing arena between conservative and liberal approaches. The current challenge is to develop a 'third way' which moves beyond this conservative-liberal opposition and which is not based on an essentially punitive stance or one which concentrates on addressing the worst and most obvious excesses of prostitution, but tends to avoid addressing the wider social and economic and political structures which produce these harms. If we can effectively identify harms, then why not aim to remove them rather than be satisfied with merely reducing them.

Although harm minimisation is a risk-based, forward-looking approach it gravitates towards a policy of normalisation and acceptance both the involvement of women in prostitution as well as the 'demand' of clients. Any form of moralising is explicitly avoided and terms like 'prostitute' are conspicuously avoided because of its stigmatising potential. Within this quasi-medicalised approach to social problems explicit moral judgements are replaced with implicit ones based on scientific or medical views of 'good' and 'bad' behaviour.

It is in relation to the issue of drugs that harm minimisation has been most closely associated. As Pat O'Malley (2004) has pointed out harm minimisation discourses on drugs do not necessarily make dependence itself a target of governance. The widespread use of methadone, although promoted as a way out of dependency, often creates another form of dependency, for not only does it involve the continued dependence on opiates, with the associated biochemical risks, but produces a form of dependency that often proves more difficult to break. As in the UK, the adoption of methadone programmes for injecting heroin users while reducing the risk associated with injection and drug adulteration has resulted in an aging cohort of dependent methadone users (Parker et al. 1998). This development, of course, not only sustains the dependency and addiction of this cohort but also perpetrators' need for drug agencies to monitor and supervise their 'clients'.

Parallels can be drawn between the harm reduction approaches which have been adopted in relation to prostitution and that adopted in relation to the homeless. The policy of providing hostels, soup kitchens and other services designed to help the homeless has resulted in a strategy which maintains many people in a state of homelessness rather than providing the type of training, medical and psychiatric care which would be necessary to get people off the streets and into mainstream society. It is estimated that it costs approximately £60,000 per annum to maintain a homeless person in a hostel in London. Instead of sustaining people in a state of homelessness and dependency, John Bird, the founder of 'Big Issue', has argued that a more comprehensive strategy could effectively transform the lives of many homeless people and that such a strategy could be cost-effective in the long term (Bird 2006). As with the homeless, it is suggested that getting people off the streets and out of destitution requires an approach which can provide the support necessary to help people leave prostitution, rather than creating new forms of dependency.

We are unfortunately a long way from providing these necessary services but some more progressive and dynamic local authorities are moving towards offering more comprehensive and relevant forms of provision. While we are waiting for such provision the most constructive response is to give encouragement to women who want to leave prostitution and provide them with a systematic and coherent exiting strategy.

The desire to exit

There is some evidence to suggest that many of the women involved in prostitution, particularly those working on the street, would like to leave but they often find exiting difficult. Melissa Farley (1998) claims that many of those who work on the streets in America are dissatisfied with their lives and express a desire to leave prostitution. Canadian-based research found that over 90 per cent of the women surveyed viewed prostitution neither as a choice nor a profession, but rather want help in getting out of prostitution (Audet and Carrier 2006). Similarly, research projects that have been carried out in the UK have found that although women often express anxiety and uncertainty about leaving prostitution nearly all of the women surveyed envisage a future free from prostitution (Rickard 2001).

Research on the development of exiting strategies in North London found that all the women surveyed had considered leaving prostitution (Bradford 2005). The same report emphasises that many of these women are unable or unlikely to leave prostitution by themselves and would need some degree of support:

> From the interviews with women attending the SHOC drop-in service it was apparent that almost all had considered exiting from sex work at some point in their sex work career, and this was even true of those who had come to sex work recently. The prospect of exiting sex work for many, however, seemed a daunting process as the life changes that they would have to undergo in this process would be far reaching. It was clear to many that the decision to exit sex work was not a question of ceasing to go out on the street at night, but would involve the resolution of many other issues in their life . . . Thus, when women were questioned about exiting sex work, women were understandably dubious about their own ability to make such life changes and presented few coherent strategies for the process of exiting sex work. This being said, the desire to exit sex work, in some cases, remained very strong.
>
> (Bradford 2005: 34)

The report emphasises the need for the development of a proactive and supportive strategy which could help these women achieve their objective.

Developing exiting strategies

If we are to move beyond an essentially reactive harm reduction approach we need to be able to offer women involved in prostitution a package of support that is both attractive and viable. Such a package will necessarily be holistic and structured and based on a realistic assessment of the difficulties and obstacles of exiting.

The Glasgow based 'Routes Out' project has developed a proactive and integrated approach which is based on the premise that involvement in prostitution is intrinsically harmful to women. Before the 'Routes Out' project was established there had been some inter-agency working based on a harm reduction model, which displayed little interest in either preventing women entering prostitution or providing support for women who wanted to leave. Prostitution had been viewed as a 'lifestyle option' rather than an issue of social exclusion and survival. Adopting a strategic approach to the issue of prostitution the Intervention Team work with vulnerable girls and young women, respond to women wishing to exit prostitution and work with relevant agencies to make mainstream services more accessible. Working with a model based on engagement, counselling, and cognitive behavioural therapy techniques designed to change thinking and address harm, the team work closely with a drug treatment agency and have developed a three stage model of intervention based on Judith Herman's (1992) therapeutic model. This model involves:

> Stage One was done in conjunction with the referring agency, building safety, giving practical help and developing trust. In stage two, women were encouraged to address emotional issues connected to harm. Stage three involved women moving on to whatever they had set up as their goals. Timing was long term; it was felt to be important to proceed at the women's pace.
>
> (Swift 2005: 3)

The intervention culminates in an exit interview as women improve their mental and physical health and become drug free. In many cases, these early stages of intervention involve improving the women's self-belief while increasing their skills and confidence. It also involves accessing social, education and work activities as well as rebuilding relationships with families and children. In general, the objective of the intervention involves helping women address their emotional, social and economic issues with the long term aim of helping women to cease their involvement in prostitution altogether.

There are three important features of the approach adopted by the 'Routes Out' initiative. First, women's basic needs have to be met before they can exit prostitution. Second, there is also a distinction made between 'exiting' and 'stopping'. 'Stopping' is defined as being stable or no longer being actively involved in prostitution. 'Exiting' on the other hand, is defined as being drug free, re-integrated with family contact, being in education, training or work, having a secure home, gaining financial independence and developing a new sense of self. Third, a recognition that there was a high probability of a relapse during the intervention. Although the 'Routes Out' project is committed to an inter-agency approach there are problems of coordination between different agencies as some of the referral agencies involved are not committed to an exiting strategy and remain tied to a harm reduction approach.

Between 2001–04 the total number of referrals to the project was 229 – of these a minimum of 41 were reported to have exited prostitution, although the data is incomplete. There is also no data on the number of women stopping prostitution. The team, however, is small and is only able to handle a limited number of cases. In some cases the women are engaged with the programme over a long period of time. Equally as important as the number of successes are the reasons why women do not complete stage three of the programme. The reasons given were the continuation of drug taking, homelessness, or unrealistic or non-specific expectations on referral. Those who were more likely to successfully complete the programme were found to be those who received positive support from family or friends, have an absence of serious mental health issues or have access to secure accommodation. It was also found that those who had stopped drug abuse improved their physical and mental health, and in some cases engaged in work or education, and were able to rebuild their normal day-to-day lives.

The survey of exiting projects conducted by Hester and Westmarland (2004) found similar results and concluded that an important aspect of exiting projects is to get to know women in order to develop trust. The development of outreach work, drop-in services and one-to-one support were also identified as being critical ways of targeting support to fit individual needs. Hester and Westmarland also emphasised the need for exiting strategies to be consistent, continuous, comprehensive and holistic. It is also necessary, they argue, that exiting strategies go beyond a harm minimisation approach. In their review of five different exiting projects they point out that:

> With regard to exiting the profiles of the women using these five projects showed that most of the women were trying to exit prostitution or had tried in the past on one or more occasions (69%, 128/186). Less than a third had never tried to exit. If women did not want to or feel ready to exit prostitution, the support interventions worked as a form of harm minimisation. The fact that the majority of women had attempted to exit also highlights the need for projects to support women towards exiting prostitution, rather than focusing solely on harm minimisation.
>
> (Hester and Westmarland 2004: 85)

Their review, however, indicates that these projects achieved a relatively low level of exiting, poor evaluations and in some cases a low level of commitment to help women leave prostitution. It is, however, difficult they suggest to effectively evaluate exiting strategies because of the vagueness of the definitions of key concepts, the lack of systematic data collection and monitoring, the small sample sizes and response rates, lack of detailed evaluation of the role of specific elements in the projects, and finally the lack of recognition in many projects of the role of coercion by pimps and partners.

One of the few projects which have taken into account the role of the coercion from pimps/partners and boyfriends is the Maze Marigold project based in Tower Hamlets and Hackney in London. This project involves recognition of the major role which coercion and intimidation can play in keeping women involved in prostitution and is linked to the provision of domestic violence support services. Emergency housing as well as specialist counselling on abuse is also provided to assist women. Interestingly, the women who have exited prostitution have, in many cases, been re-housed outside of the area where they had been working.

The Stoke-on-Trent Peer Support initiative has been developed which provides a structured approach and claims a relatively high level of success in relation to exiting (see Hester and Westmarland), although since 2001 it has focused on providing one-to-one support rather than peer support. Based on an individually tailored care plan the approach adopted in Stoke-on-Trent assists the women to examine all aspects of their lives including their drug dependency, finances, housing, children and relationships with others. Based on this programme women can begin accessing the relevant services including peer support group sessions. A fast track drugs programme has also been developed alongside training, re-housing and in conjunction with the provision of alternative employment opportunities. Stabilising drug use is seen as a crucial first step in developing an exiting strategy and in some cases the women's boyfriends/partners/pimps may also be referred to fast track drug services.

Other projects which have developed exiting initiatives in the UK include the Streetreach Project in Doncaster which aims to help women off the streets and into work. The project has developed in partnership with Reed, a recruitment company, who provide employment advice. Between 2001–04 over 50 women have been helped back into mainstream work through the Reed partnership. These jobs range from beauty therapy to work in the travel industry (Salman 2004).

In general, most projects argue for a holistic approach to exiting and recognise that piecemeal and patchy interventions are unlikely to be effective with this vulnerable group. The question however arises of what supports and services need to be provided in such a 'holistic' strategy and what are the priorities and most appropriate order of intervention. These issues become relevant when we think about the role of drug treatment programmes in relation to exiting. Because drug addiction is in many areas the most visible aspect of street prostitution, and because problematic drug use is seen as a the main driver of this process, there is a tendency to concentrate on developing a drug treatment programme which is sometimes seen as a 'solution' in itself, rather than a first step in developing an exiting strategy. For other women, however, issues such as housing, physical and mental health, may be equally important in terms of stabilising their lives. The concentration on drug treatment programmes and the view that other issues are secondary and subordinate may explain why the success and completion rate of a number of different drug treatment programmes is relatively low (Hester and Westmarland 2004).

Drawing on the work that has been carried out to date by some of the more successful and committed agencies it is possible to develop a structured approach to exiting. On the basis that agencies concerned have a clear and unequivocal commitment to helping women exit from prostitution the following model would seem to be appropriate:

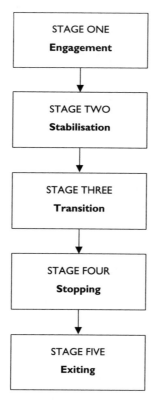

Figure 5.1 Exiting from prostitution.

The initial stage of engagement involves building trust and developing a supportive relationship. Stage two is a critical stage of stabilisation which involves the cessation of problems of drug use either by reducing or ceasing drug consumption, providing residential accommodation with support advocacy and addressing other factors such as coercion from partners/boyfriends which serve to undermine the ability of women to control their own lives. For this stage to be more generally effective more fast-track drug treatment programmes need to be available and significantly more residential provision with the appropriate facilities need to be provided in key areas.

Stage three is probably the longest phase and will involve providing a range of services including training, counselling, assistance with health and financial problems, further drug treatment, re-establishing contacts with children and families following the provision of long-term accommodation, probably in an area away from that in which the person has previously worked. Stage four involves ceasing to be involved in prostitution and beginning to establish an alternative lifestyle. Stage five involves developing a new non-prostitute identity and moving on.

It is probably the case that if a well funded and user-friendly exiting strategy was made available in different areas the majority of those currently involved in street prostitution would leave within a five year period. Such a structured but flexible package needs to be presented proactively, rather than place the onus on those involved in prostitution to request such services. If the women involved in prostitution do not want to take up the offer there should be no compulsion, but if we work with the presumption that the majority of women working on the street are disaffected, disorganised and damaged then such an approach could provide a way out for many women.

A strategy of this type involves a long-term continuous programme. Moving through these five steps can take anything from a few months to a few years. For this reason funding needs to be long term. It is also important that agencies need to be specialist and dedicated to exiting. There is little point funding those agencies that include exiting as an 'add on' in order to increase their own profile or to secure funding but have no real interest in developing effective strategies.

In sum, a review of these various projects suggests that the key components in developing an effective strategy involves:

- Moving beyond a harm minimisation approach and developing a more proactive approach;
- Developing an effective set of interventions which require an approach which is structured, flexible, and continuous;
- Pursuing a holistic approach which is able to address a wide range of issues that can be tailored to the needs of individual women;
- The ability to relocate women, where possible, in areas away from those where they have been involved in prostitution.

What these various approaches suggest is that a tailored and structured package linked to the needs of women, which is flexible but comprehensive is potentially the most effective way of helping women leave prostitution. Such an approach was developed to good effect in Sweden in the 1970s and has subsequently become a major point of reference for those who want to help women leave prostitution. This initiative is known as the Malmo Project. It was directed primarily, but not exclusively, towards helping women leave prostitution. It involved a form of outreach and was able to assist women with economic and housing problems as well as with training, employment and educational opportunities. It also put women in contact with psychologists and mainstream services and helped with legal problems. It also helped women who had issues with pimps. The project provided concrete assistance and recognised that if women were to be helped out of prostitution there were a number of issues that needed to be addressed. The project workers used the media to advertise the project and to attract women. The evaluation of the project suggested that it provided a successful approach and 55 per cent of the women were reported to have not prostituted themselves since contact with the project. Some 14 per cent had sporadically engaged in prostitution after contact with the project but eventually quit. These results indicate that over 70 per cent of the women who engaged in the project left prostitution either straightaway or eventually. Between 1974 and 1981 the number of known prostitutes in Malmo decreased from 300 to 60 (Hoigard and Finstad 1992).

The significance of the Malmo Project was that it provided an holistic and integrated approach to exiting. It provided advice on a range of issues simultaneously and consistently. It involved not only the provision of training, but also financial assistance where necessary. Similar strategies have been adopted in Norway to good effect and the message is that a well-organised and well-resourced intervention which is sustained over a period of time can be very effective in helping women to exit prostitution.

Conclusion

It is indicative that it is only recently that there has been a concerted effort to develop exiting strategies. This development has been initiated by various local and central government organisations, who have come to realise that many women – particularly those working on the street – would like to leave prostitution, but find themselves trapped in various ways. It is unfortunate, however, that most of the agencies in the UK, which aim to support prostitutes, provide a response that is largely reactive and linked to a harm minimisation approach. Many of the representatives of these agencies view prostitution as an essentially positive lifestyle choice rather than seeing the women as victims or survivors. Consequently, the interest among some agencies and organisations in relation to exiting can be token and responses tend not to be joined up. Moreover, there is always a danger, as Stephen Farrell (2005) notes in his study on desistance, that practitioners spend more time talking to clients about their problems rather than acting directly to solve them. It is indicative that in the UK there are few surveys asking women involved in prostitution whether they would like to leave and developing a structured but individually tailored strategy to help them get out.

The experience of the Malmo Project provides an instructive model of intervention. This approach involves a comprehensive package of interventions, which is aimed at providing the necessary measures for women to exit prostitution. In line with the Malmo Project the 'best practice' from British projects confirms that an effective approach needs to be structured, holistic, long-term, individually tailored and integrated.

It is probably the case that, as more effective and user-friendly exiting packages are developed, more women will sign up to them. As the number of those working on the streets in urban centres in different parts of the UK are stabilising or decreasing we have probably reached a point where it is more cost-effective to develop comprehensive exiting strategies rather than continually recycling women through the criminal justice system. As noted above, many of the women who work on the streets are multiple victims and also victims of a welfare system that has systematically failed them. Just as the government in England and Wales has recently come to realise that in dealing with those who have been in prison or who are designated as 'prolific and persistent offenders' it makes more sense to spend money developing *inclusive* resettlement packages rather than continually recycling individuals through the criminal justice system, so it is the case with prostitution (see Dawson and Cuppleditch 2007; Lewis et al. 2003).

Chapter 6

The politics of prostitution

Introduction

There are four general policy options that have been developed in different countries and in different periods to regulate prostitution. These are regulationism, decriminalisation, legalisation, and prohibition. At the most general level the policy debate has centred around the advantages and disadvantages of each of these policy options. Although it is possible, and indeed necessary, to examine these options in their essential forms, the selection of the most appropriate option is complicated by a number of considerations.

The first is that in practical terms different counties or states may be characterised as having a policy of 'decriminalisation' or 'regulationism' but in fact operate with a mix of different policies operating at different levels. For example, England and Wales is normally characterised as 'regulationist', which means that prostitution itself is not criminalised, but a range of interventions operate to address issues of public order, nuisance, exploitation and the like. However, there exists a substantial network of 'saunas' and 'massage parlours' across the country which are licensed by the local state and everyone, apart from the people who work in the licensing department, know that they are brothels which are formally illegal but widely tolerated. Similarly, France is normally described as an 'abolitionist' country, because it closed down its state controlled brothels in 1946 and officially refuses to accept that prostitution is a legitimate occupation, although it still seeks to tax women involved in prostitution (Allwood 2004). Moreover, New Zealand is frequently characterised as introducing a policy of decriminalisation in 2003 but the new legislation was principally directed at creating a system of licensing and regulation and in effect introduced a hybrid system of legalisation and decriminalisation (Jordan 2005).

The second qualification, which arises when considering how prostitution is regulated in different locations, is that in most countries there are normally two or three tiers of formal regulation operating at the federal, provincial and municipal levels. In Canada, for example, prostitution is generally dealt with by the federal government under the Criminal Code. However, issues of public order and nuisance, which have increasingly come to be associated with street prostitution, have also been regulated by municipal and provincial governments (Jeffreys 2004). In other countries like Britain there is an inter-play between local government and central government with local govern-ment playing a significant role in dealing with issues of disorder and licensing as well as implementing multi-agency initiatives.

The third consideration in characterising certain countries as 'prohibition-ist' or as 'regulationist' is that there are often considerable regional variations in how prostitution is regulated. Australia, for example, is often referred to as a country that has developed a policy of legalisation, but in fact it is only in certain states – New South Wales, Victoria, Queensland and the Northern Territory – that have adopted this approach, while the other states operate with different policies. This observation has two implications. The first is that we must be careful of talking about 'the Australian experience' and second is that we must remain sensitive to how policies in some states may be sustained or alternatively have effects on neighbouring regions.

The fourth and related consideration is that we should avoid describing countries or even certain states as essentially 'regulationist' or 'abolitionist'. The experience of the last decade is that there are a number of countries, which have undergone fundamental policy shifts changing from one dominant form of policy to another over time. Scandinavian countries, for example, have in recent years changed their policies on prostitution quite radically. Thus:

> Whereas Denmark, Norway and Sweden until recently had almost iden-tical legal approaches to prostitution, as outlined above, the last couple of years have taken Denmark in one direction, Sweden in another while Norway remains in the middle. In 1999, prostitution became fully legalised in Denmark (though pimping, procuring and buying sex from minors were illegal). In Sweden, buying sex became an offence on 1st January 1999.
>
> (Skilbrei 2001: 68)

The Netherlands over the past century has changed from being abolitionist, which involved outlawing brothels, and making pimping a criminal offence, to a policy of regulationism in the mid-twentieth century which limited prostitution to certain areas. More recently, the Netherlands has embraced a policy of legalisation which aims to turn prostitution into a legitimate form of work and at the same time cleanse and control the sex industry (Outshoorn 2004).

A fifth consideration is that the general policies of 'decriminalisation' or 'legalisation' are endorsed and implemented to different degrees and in dif-ferent ways in different locations. As we shall see, for example in relation to decriminalisation, it can involve calls for removing all the legislation directed towards prostitution or it may only involve calling for the removal of the legislation which is directed towards the women involved in prostitution.

A final point that should be noted is that there is frequent slippage and overlap in the use of the basic categories. Thus the term 'regulationism' is used by some authors as synonymous with 'abolitionism' (because some countries have closed down brothels and operate a form of regulationism), while abolitionism is sometimes used to refer to the abolition of brothels and in other cases the abolition of laws controlling prostitution (Allwood 2004; Barry 1995; Corbin 1990). There is also frequent confusion between decriminalisation and legalisation since both approaches involve the removal or restructuring of laws against prostitution.

In general, it can be seen that the various options – regulationism, decriminalisation, legalisation and prohibition – are rarely implemented in their pure forms and that there is nearly always a mix of policies in place in different countries and this mix can change over time. Thus these four main options should be treated as 'ideal types', which signal a policy direction that in practice will be subject to qualifications, overlaps and contradictions.

The recognition of the various considerations alerts us to the complexity of these debates as well as differences between the rhetoric and the reality of policy. At the same time it serves as a reminder against making sweeping generalisations and the tendency to offer quick fixes. Like the debate on drugs, the debate on prostitution is something of a quagmire, often underpinned by suppressed moralisms and unexamined myths and misconceptions, some of which have been referred to above. Having outlined these qualifications it is necessary to examine current policy options. In doing so it has become an established practice to draw on the experience of different countries that have adopted these dominant policy positions, although again we must be cautious in attempting to simply transfer policies between different countries, since their adoption and operation is often bound up with particular national characteristics, circumstances and cultural norms.

Regulationism

Regulationism emerged in the mid-nineteenth century and was associated in Britain with the work of William Acton (1857) and in France with that of Parent-Duchalet (1836). The main aim of regulationism is not the suppression of prostitution in general but the control of the excesses, abuses and disorder that is often associated with it. For that reason prostitution within a regulationist framework is not itself illegal and the objective is to manage the unwanted and undesirable consequences of its operation.

Regulationism eschews an overt moralism or fatalism and believes that prostitution can be regulated and administered in such a way that it is possible to reduce its negative associations. While not endorsing or promoting prostitution it formally remains agnostic if not ambivalent about its desirability and acceptability. In many countries such as the UK regulationism has been affected by waves of abolitionism, which has sought historically to close down brothels. This post-abolitionist form of regulationism will be referred to as neo-regulationism.

Regulationism also involves a form of state obligated care and control of prostitution. It sees prostitution as predominantly a social issue and gravitates towards communitarianism rather than liberalism. Its concerns are mainly centred around prostitution rather than the prostitute. Its aim is therefore not to criminalise the prostitute per se or to object in principle to the acts of selling or purchasing sexual services. Rather, its aim is to divest prostitution of its less desirable attributes and to compensate in some cases for the social and individual effects of prostitution.

Its approach is based on evidence and analysis including an assessment of public opinion. However, its main focus has tended to be on the street trade and on 'public women' and advocates the need for both tolerance and supervision of those who work on the streets. There is an emphasis on suppression and surveillance. In its early formulation, regulationism according to Corbin (1990), consisted of 'damming up, containing and canalising excess by efficient administrative means, without intervention of the legal system'. By the early twentieth century neo-regulationism came to rely more on policing methods and legal controls.

At the end of the nineteenth century the logic of regulationism was fractured by the abolitionist movement, which campaigned for the closure of licensed brothels. This campaign was more successful in England than in France, although both have been described as abolitionist countries. In fact, in the UK, after the closing down of brothels in the nineteenth century the dominant policy shifted to a form of neo-regulationism, which was most forcibly articulated in the Wolfenden Report (1957). The Wolfenden Report was seen as a path-breaking publication that has set the basic policy agenda in the UK for the past 50 years. It was widely seen as providing a more liberal approach, in that it was not concerned with the morality of prostitution as such but aimed to rationalise the resources directed towards the control of prostitution, while increasing the certainty of conviction. It was the visible manifestation of street prostitution that was its primary focus. The authors of the report clearly outlined its general approach:

> We clearly recognise that the laws of any society must be acceptable to the general moral sense of the community. But we are not charged to enter matters of private moral conduct, except in so far as they directly affect the public good. In this field, its (the law's) function as we see it to preserve public order and decency, to protect the citizen from what is offensive and injurious and to provide sufficient safeguards against exploitation and corruption.

(Wolfenden Report 1957: 9–10)

The point of reference for the Committee was the sensibilities of the 'average citizen' and visitors to the Capital. The Committee felt that they were reflecting public opinion and providing a practical response to the increasing number of women seen working on the streets in the UK in the 1950s. The policing of prostitution had always been hampered according to the Wolfenden Report by the problem of gathering evidence and finding witnesses who would testify. It suggested that to overcome this obstacle the need to prove annoyance should be removed, while increasing police discretion through the introduction of a cautioning system. Because convictions could now be based on police evidence alone, cases were rarely contested and after the Street Offences Act 1959, which was largely based on the Wolfenden Committee's recommendations, the visibility of street prostitution was reduced, while more clandestine and commercialised forms of prostitution were encouraged.

In relation to prostitution, the Wolfenden Report proposed a substantial increase in the maximum penalty for persistent soliciting, progressively higher fines for repeated offences, with an ultimate maximum of three months imprisonment, which was increased from 14 days. The focus of the report was the visibility of women soliciting rather than the activities of male clients. It was claimed that the 'women do parade themselves more habitually and openly than their prospective customers'. Although Wolfenden was seen in some quarters as a radical and even permissive report it in fact perpetuated a moral double standard. As Stuart Hall has argued:

> The key to the Wolfenden Report's 'permissiveness' and the real index as to the specific character and the limits of its reformism is thus the tendency it exhibited towards the *privatisation* of selective aspects of sexual conduct. The philosophical rationale which it employed was the distinction between crime and sin, illegality and immorality – a blurred and indistinct boundary within the English Criminal Law which by selective reiteration Wolfenden immeasurably strengthened.
>
> (Hall 1980: 13)

Wolfenden articulated according to Hall a new 'moral economy' based on a selective resurrection of legal utilitarianism. Thus Wolfenden presented a bifurcated strategy which on one side involved stricter penalties and more systematic control while advocating greater freedom and leniency on the other. The underlying current of Wolfenden, Hall argues, was a campaign to return women to the home and to promote the family and marriage. The visibility of prostitution, it is suggested, undermined ideologies of 'femininity' and 'sexuality' as well as women's 'traditional' domestic role. What was significant about the report was the identification of the female prostitute as a specific category or person – a common prostitute – rather than someone who had engaged in a specific act.

Although the Wolfenden Committee saw their primary objective as providing a 'solution' to the perceived problem of street prostitution it elaborated a revised commitment to the issues of commercialisation and exploitation. The legislation regarding commercialisation and exploitation had been formulated at the end of the nineteenth century and had, with a few revisions, remained largely intact during the first half of the twentieth century. Its main elements included legislation dealing with 'living off immoral earnings' directed mainly at pimps and procurers as well as controlling the use of rented premises for the purpose of prostitution; the suppression of brothels through legislation prohibiting more than one woman working from a designated premises; the protection of those under the age of consent from 'unlawful carnal intercourse' and sanctioning those who attempted to procure a woman to be a 'common prostitute'.

To some extent, Wolfenden consolidated much of the exiting legislation, which aimed to protect women, deter pimps, and suppress brothels. The legalisation of brothels was firmly rejected as it was seen as likely to promote trafficking and increase the number of underage young girls involved in prostitution. However, the Committee did anticipate that the reduction of the street trade would probably expand into the 'call girl' system and the growth of those working from the private flats.

Attitudes towards 'ponces' and 'pimps' were moderated and the Committee expressed the view that the violent pimp was a thing of the past and that women were not 'entirely passive', while suggesting that many of those who live on the earnings of prostitution are often partners rather than exploiters. Consequently the Committee concluded that the two-year maximum sentence for living off the earnings of prostitution should remain unchanged. Similarly, in relation to procuring the Committee did not recommend any changes in the law.

In sum, the Committee expressed the view that as long as prostitution remained privatised and invisible to the general public and thereby did not cause nuisance and offence, and was not carried out in premises involving more than one person (a brothel) it could be tolerated. The legacy of Wolfenden and the legislation which it inspired was to limit the visibility of prostitution and to develop a more efficient method for prosecuting the women who worked on the streets, while inadvertently encouraging more privatised and commercialised forms of prostitution.

Decriminalisation

Decriminalisation involves the removal of all or some of the laws relating to prostitution. The arguments for decriminalisation have been presented by two main groups. On the one hand, the international feminist movement in the 1970s and 1980s called for the abolition of laws directed at the female prostitute and argued that these laws were discriminatory, unjust and often counterproductive. In contrast to this position of 'partial' decriminalisation there has been a call for more wide ranging forms of decriminalisation, and even total decriminalisation, which have come from liberals and libertarians who have argued that prostitution is not the law's business and that free market principles should be allowed to operate in relation to the sex industry. In this more extreme form of decriminalisation it is argued that even legislation designed to control exploitation should be removed. Although there is some overlap between these versions of decriminalisation – particularly in relation to arguments used against the legal control of women involved in prostitution – there are also significant differences and tensions.

One point of agreement is the perceived discriminatory nature of the law and its enforcement. Historically, legislation has concentrated on penalising the female prostitute while largely ignoring the role of the client. Nineteenth century public order legislation which aims to criminalise 'soliciting for the purpose of prostitution' has been constructed as a gender-specific offence (as only women 'solicit') and reinforces the dominant ideology that prostitution is 'supply' driven rather than 'demand' led.

Those arguing for decriminalisation in the UK have often focused on what are seen as the limitations of neo-regulationism as outlined in the Wolfenden Report (1957). They object to the fact that women can be arrested and prosecuted as a result of police evidence alone, which virtually removes the right to defence. Appearing in court as a 'common prostitute' there is, it is argued, a presumption of guilt with a very high probability of receiving a fine (Matthews 1986). Although there has been a noticeable shift over the last decade away from the arrest and prosecution of women for soliciting and a greater focus on the 'kerb crawling' of male clients, this does not necessarily provide a form of greater equality because the situations and motivations of the female prostitutes and the male clients are very different. Thus, it is argued that criminalising both does not create greater equality but compounds existing inequalities.

Once a woman has a criminal record for a prostitution-related offence it reinforces her marginalisation and vulnerability, on the one hand, while making it more difficult for her to leave prostitution and find legitimate employment on the other. The increased marginalisation itself produces a number of other undesirable effects. It increases the vulnerability of women to abuse and assault from both clients and pimps/partners since these perpetrators believe that they can commit these acts with a degree of impunity. If women are to provide evidence and report those who abuse, coerce and assault them then their quasi-illegal status acts as a major barrier. Arguably, the illegal status of the women increases the likelihood that the only relationships she will be able to maintain will be with those who see her as an easy source of money (Davis and Shaffer 1994). The criminalisation of the women involved in prostitution and the objective of rendering them 'invisible' can also create difficulties in accessing necessary health services.

There are also issues of cost. The cost to the taxpayer of the various criminal justice agencies which police prostitution is substantial. The rounding up of the 'usual suspects' and processing them through the courts, and in some cases prisons, does little to address the fundamental problem. This money could be more usefully spent developing support and exiting packages.

A further objection to the criminalisation of 'soliciting' is the mobilising of appropriate sanctions. Up until the 1980s in England and Wales 'soliciting' was an imprisonable offence. Increasingly, it became recognised that this sanction was too severe, inappropriate and in many cases counterproductive since it further marginalised the women concerned. Subsequently, working women convicted of 'soliciting' have been dealt with by fines, which in some cases are paid off by serving short terms of imprisonment. Again, the use of fines are widely seen as counterproductive and it is usually argued that this sanction 'forces' women back into 'the game' in order to earn the money to pay off the fine.

The use of the fine may have been justified to some degree when dealing with what we have referred to above as 'economic prostitutes'. That is, those who engage in prostitution to earn a living, to supplement their income or to deal with pressing financial problems. But as the composition of street prostitution shifts towards drug addicted, disorganised and damaged women in the UK and other countries the use of fines appears to be increasingly inappropriate. Indeed, the unavailability of an appropriate sanction for women who work on the streets may be one of the reasons why the police in England and Wales have dramatically decreased the number of women arrested and prosecuted in recent years and have increasingly dealt with street prostitution through spatial controls and by referring women to specialist agencies (Matthews 2005).

Increasingly, in the eyes of many observers and practitioners the women involved in street prostitution are seen more as victims than offenders who already suffer not only economic and social disadvantage, but have histories of abuse and neglect. In fact, she is commonly seen not only as a victim of circumstances but often as a 'double victim' by being propelled into a situation of quasi-illegality which maintains her in a subordinate relation to customers and pimps as well as other agents who can exploit her (Shrage 1996).

It is the perpetuation of vulnerability and the tendency to reinforce the marginalisation of the women involved in street prostitution, which is increasingly becoming the most significant argument against the continued criminalisation of those working on the streets. In relation to the growing, if under-developed, focus on exiting, the continued criminalisation of 'soliciting' provides a major obstacle by reinforcing the marginalisation and stigmatisation of the women concerned. In particular, their quasi-illegal status makes them reticent to expose those who exploit or coerce them. While the vast majority of feminists are sympathetic towards the decriminalisation of women involved in prostitution they advocate tough laws against those who exploit and abuse these women. In some cases, they are opposed to prostitution because it degrades and objectifies women while at the same time defending those women who are involved in prostitution (Barry 1998; Overall 1992; Sullivan 1995).

It could be argued that the removal of the offence of 'soliciting' and removing the quasi-legal status of prostitution would undermine the deterrent effect of the legislation. This argument may have been appropriate in periods in which the motivation for entrance into prostitution was principally economic, but as drug addiction and related problems come to be associated with entry the deterrent argument loses much of its weight. Thus, there is currently a strong if not compelling argument for the removal of the offence of soliciting and for taking a significant historic step in the regulation of prostitution. This is in fact the direction that policy is currently going in the UK, and the removal of the offence of 'soliciting' would not necessarily involve a break with regulationism, but rather provide a significant and progressive re-orientation.

The decriminalisation of soliciting, however, for many liberals does not go far enough. They argue that prostitution is a non-victim crime and that intervention is driven by a thinly veiled moralism that seeks to criminalise all forms of sexual activity which are not linked to marriage and reproduction. It is argued that prostitution is a job like any other, that prostitutes are rational agents, that pimps are in fact boyfriends/partners; while clients, with a few unfortunate exceptions, are drawn widely from across the male population and that a significant number are single, shy, disabled and older men for whom prostitution provides a form of social service.

These liberals are generally opposed to all forms of state intervention, which is seen as restricting trade and limiting individual 'freedom'. They tend only to support state intervention in the sex industry when it is seen to facilitate trade and allow individuals to operate more effectively in the market. Harm minimisation strategies function well in this respect, since this normally involves reducing impediments such as violence from clients, while providing forms of health and social support, which are seen to allow the women to function more effectively.

There is a tendency amongst liberals to normalise different aspects of prostitution. Thus the English Collective of Prostitutes (1997), for example, claim that all women are prostitutes and that the difference between those women involved in prostitution and ordinary women is that the former charge for sexual services while the latter are 'expected to do it for free'. They also argue that although prostitution may be degrading it is no worse than a number of other jobs, which women are expected to perform, except that it pays better and gives the women concerned greater independence. The barriers, however, to realising this independence are the legal controls that limit earnings, restrict trade, deter customers and stigmatise those involved.

Groups like the English Collective of Prostitutes also want to normalise and decriminalise clients. These men, it is claimed, are driven by natural impulses and tend to be lonely, single and disabled men, who are not able to engage in 'normal' sexual relations and might otherwise seek other more damaging ways to fulfil their sexual needs. Clients, it is claimed, are normal men and the proportion of the male population who visit prostitutes is considerably higher than most people assume. Consequently, those advocating total decriminalisation tend to oppose legislation that impacts upon clients. At the same time, groups like the English Collective of Prostitutes have opposed the kerb crawling legislation which was introduced in England and Wales in the mid 1980s, partly on the basis that like the legislation controlling soliciting, the legislation relating to kerb crawling is based principally on police evidence and this raises issues about the rights of defendants and the use of police discretion.

Other groups like the Scarlet Alliance in Australia want all legislation directed specifically at prostitution to be removed and argue that the sex industry should be treated as any other commercial business and subject to the same forms of regulation (Banach and Metzenrath 2000). They want to see 'sex work' as a legitimate form of employment and claim that it is legal controls that have led to the stigmatisation of those involved in prostitution. They want to remove legislation relating to 'living off the earnings of prostitution' since they argue that this 'restricts how sex workers can spend their money' and do not want controls on brothel keeping because it denies sex workers the relative economic and physical security of legal brothel work.

In these liberal and libertarian accounts, however, the role of abuse, exploitation and coercion are downplayed and the free reign of market principles is emphasised. Groups like the English Collective of Prostitutes and the Scarlet Alliance seem impervious to the informal and social forces that have historically generated the stigmatisation of those involved in prostitution. Also, there is little regard for the concerns and experiences of those living in and around red light districts. Thus, while advocating total decriminalisation the Scarlet Alliance note that 93 per cent of the public (who were surveyed in 1998 in Queensland) expressed significant opposition to street prostitution. This type of opposition as we have seen has been prevalent in the UK, Canada, America and elsewhere, yet this evidence is dismissed on the basis of dubious methodologies, conservative community attitudes and fears of police corruption.

The failure to take the attitudes of the general public seriously, particularly those that live in red light districts is politically and strategically inadequate. Thus, while it has been suggested that there are good grounds for considering the decriminalisation of soliciting, the issue of community attitudes to street prostitution needs to be addressed. These communities, which are often vulnerable and disadvantaged, also have rights to freedom of movement and security, which need to be given serious consideration. Thus advocating the decriminalisation of soliciting-related offences does not mean removing all forms of regulation and that other, more appropriate measures need to be developed to effectively protect communities.

Legalisation

The legalisation of prostitution is, superficially, an attractive option. It appears to solve some of the problems that have become associated with regulationism and seems to offer a solution to the dilemma of not criminalising prostitution per se but at the same time controlling the activities of those involved in prostitution. Legalisation offers the promise of reducing the street trade while providing a more secure environment in which women can work.

Like many of those who argue for total decriminalisation the legalisation lobby generally argue that prostitution is the oldest profession and that it 'will always be with us' and that we should take a pragmatic approach and organise it in a way which is of much greater benefit to the clients, the women, the entrepreneurs and ultimately to society. They also argue that prostitution is a legitimate occupation and that legalisation can provide the structure for safeguarding the rights of sex workers. Legalisation in line with decriminalisation is also seen as a way of avoiding moralisms and the perceived hypocrisy of regulationism, by accepting prostitution.

In essence, the legalisation of prostitution takes two forms: off street and on street. The off street form involves the establishment of state approved brothels while the on street version involves the creation of designated 'toleration zones' where street prostitution is allowed to operate freely.

The arguments for legalisation are well rehearsed and often in times of crisis, or where regulationism is seen to be failing, legalisation is often proposed as a viable alternative. One of the most attractive arguments for legalisation is its claim to locate prostitution in a controlled environment away from residential areas. The argument is often embellished with the additional claim that the establishment of brothels will reduce the level of street prostitution and will provide greater protection for the women involved from violence and coercive pimps. Besides reducing pimping it is often suggested that state-licensed establishments will reduce involvement of organised crime in the sex trade. The advocates of legalisation also claim that licensed brothels can provide regular health checks for women and thereby reduce the level of sexually transmitted diseases. In general, organising prostitution in state-licensed premises will, it is argued, provide a more congenial, safer and better controlled environment for the women involved in prostitution as well as for the clients.

There is a considerable gap between the promise and the performance of legalisation. In fact, nearly all the claims do not stand up to critical scrutiny and the establishment of brothels tends to create more problems than it solves. These problems can take different forms and two countries that have recently experimented with legalising prostitution – Australia and the Netherlands – have had two very different, but ultimately negative experiences.

In Australia, prostitution has been legalised in a number of states, including Victoria. The stated aims of legalisation were to minimise the harms associated with prostitution, stem criminal involvement and control the expansion of the industry (Sullivan and Jeffreys 2002). In the state of Victoria, the introduction of state-licensed brothels was also rationalised in terms of diminishing health risks for both women working in brothels and their clients.

Although legalisation was introduced to control the expansion of the sex industry, it produced the opposite effect. Legalisation has led to a massive expansion, with the number of legal brothels more than doubling from 40 in 1992 to 94 by 2002. This expansion has been accompanied by a dramatic increase in other sectors of the sex industry including lap dancing, phone sex, peep shows and pornography, which have all become part of the expanding multi-million dollar business. There has also been a growth in the number of illegal brothels.

The claim that legalisation would empower women and improve their working conditions has not materialised. There have been a number of cases of young girls aged between 10 and 15 being forced to work in legal brothels, while the number of trafficked women has also increased rapidly. The ready availability of brothels has encouraged widespread trafficking often in the form of 'debt bondage'. In the state of Victoria:

> We have seen that legalisation has caused all sections of the industry to flourish. There are now many more illegal brothels than legal and grounds to believe that Victoria is the focal point of a large trafficking industry as well. Legalisation has also created a new funding revenue stream for the state that is now difficult to give up. Legalisation has proved to be the signal to the business interests to come in and develop the territory. Traffickers, it seems, prefer to operate where there are brothels to place their goods without fear of harassment, raising the question of what form of regulation of prostitution is best suited to decreasing the 'traffic of women'.
>
> (Sullivan and Jeffreys 2002: 146)

The adoption of a legalisation strategy in the Netherlands has worked out in a very different way. After introducing legal brothels in 2000 the Dutch authorities are currently in the process of closing down of many of these premises. It is estimated that there has been a 50 per cent decrease in the number of legal establishments and a consequent increase in the number of illegal establishments, often taking the form of Thai 'massage parlours'. The reasons for this sudden and unexpected decline are fivefold.

First, the plan to introduce paid employment for the women working in these establishments has been strenuously resisted by the entrepreneurs who run them. Organisations like Red Thread have campaigned for decent working conditions and proper conditions of employment, but those who own and run these brothels are not particularly interested in providing good working conditions for the women. Second, the arrangement was that the owners would pay tax, and keep proper records and books. The entrepreneurs running these establishments are, however, reluctant to pay tax and prefer to run illegal establishments where they are not subject to formal financial controls. Third, the local authority has been concerned about the links between brothel owners and organised crime and have consequently refused to issue licences to some owners. Fourth, the women working in these establishments and the groups who support them have complained about the working conditions and the restrictive nature of the contracts issued. There are reports of abuse and long working days. Some of the women work in what Red Thread (2006) describe as 'slavery like conditions' in which women are found to live in the workplace and are 'dependent on the operator'. Fifth, the clients are being sensitised to the probability that women are being trafficked and are asked to report brothels where they suspect trafficked women are being used. This has made some clients feel uncomfortable about their activities and encouraged them to provide useful information to the police. A similar initiative has been suggested in the UK (Cowan 2006).

In many ways, the experience of the Netherlands is more damning indictment of legalisation than that of Victoria since legalisation appears to be failing on all fronts. The entrepreneurs clearly do not want to run a legitimate tax-paying business or to provide good working conditions. Rather, they are more comfortable in the illegal economy where they are less accountable and able to treat the women who work in these establishments contemptuously.

It has also been suggested that the growth of the internet as well as illegal brothels means that the licensed brothels are facing increased competition (Strijbosch 2006). In 2005, the red light district in Arnhem was closed down and all the signs are that the brothels in Amsterdam will continue to decrease in relation both to the number of premises and the volume of trade.

Apart from the problems arising from legalisation in Australia and the Netherlands there are some general issues that are raised by the policy of legalisation. One of the main issues is that legalisation is seen as an endorsement of prostitution giving a green light to all those who either want to engage in it as well as to pimps, procurers and entrepreneurs. The state itself has been identified as acting like a pimp since in effect it 'lives off immoral earnings'. At the same time, however, as encouraging the growth of illegal brothels state authorities clamp down on the illegal trade, including the street trade as well as other forms of competition, which are not state sanctioned.

Thus, on the one hand, the state appears to be saying that practicing prostitution is acceptable while simultaneously sanctioning those who engage in prostitution but operate outside of the official system.

Thus in countries like Germany, which operate legal brothels, there are periodic clampdowns on the street prostitutes who operate in towns like Hamburg. Rather than reduce the scale of street prostitution legalisation encourages the expansion of the street trade. It is also erroneous to believe that the expansion of brothels will lead to a reduction of the street trade, as women are encouraged to move off street. Prostitution is a highly differentiated occupation and the type of personal organisation required to work in brothels is not a characteristic of many of the women who work on the streets. It is also a requirement in the majority of the brothels that women are not problematic drug users. At the same time, most of the women who work on the streets do not want to offer the type of commitment and routinisation which is normally required of women who work in these commercialised sex establishments. Women involved in street prostitution point out that they have an element of choice in selecting customers and in the range of sexual activities that they are willing to perform. One frequent complaint, however, from the women who work in brothels, legal or illegal, is that they are not able to refuse the demands of the customer if they want to remain working in these establishments. In this respect women working in brothels have less choice and less freedom than their street-based counterparts.

The claim that brothels offer the opportunity for regular medical inspections for those who work in them overlooks the fact that since such checks are normally carried out once a week, or fortnightly, this does not prevent the transmission of sexually transmitted diseases in the interim period. Moreover, the health checks are not given to the clients, who may be the source of infection, and therefore the health checks are inevitably of limited value and can lead to complacency and a false sense of security.

One of the frequent claims made in relation to the establishment of legal brothels is that they provide a safer and less violent environment for women. However, the evidence from Australia and the Netherlands is that the spread of legal brothels has been accompanied an increase in certain forms of violence. Thus:

> Violence against women in prostitution does not seem to have decreased in the Netherlands or Victoria since legalisation and there are even suggestions that it has increased. A report by the Australian Institute of Criminology in 1990 found that many prostitutes in legal brothels were at high risk of violence. Research in 1994 by an NGO found that a significant percentage of women felt unsafe with customers most or some of the time. The Prostitutes Collective of Victoria (PCV) was receiving up to 15 reports of rape and violence against prostitutes weekly. Also, many of these women in illegally run brothels in Victoria did not report to police,

either for fear of being charged with a prostitution-related offence or because they already had outstanding fines and were afraid of being jailed.

(Bindel and Kelly 2003:16)

The claim that legal establishments are violence-free and provide a safe environment for the women is mistaken. As Melissa Farley (2004) has argued: 'it is a cruel lie to suggest that decriminalisation or legalisation will protect anyone in prostitution' and she argues that whatever its legal status there is much evidence that prostitution causes considerable harm to the women involved. Similarly, Janice Raymond (2004) has pointed out that women working in brothels often have little choice over the type and number of clients they have to deal with or the type of sexual service that they are required to provide.

Even if it were the case that legal brothels promoted a cleaner and safer environment for the women concerned, the age span of women involved in these establishments tends to be limited, and once the women become too old or begin suffering from ill health, drug problems or develop mental health problems the likelihood is that they will be removed from the legal brothels. In countries in which the number of brothels increases significantly and the sex industry becomes more competitive the likelihood is that the turnover of women working in brothels will become greater and many of the discarded women will seek to make a living on the streets – thereby fuelling the (illegal) street trade.

Research has shown that the legalisation of prostitution does not diminish the stigma attached to prostitution. Because of the need to negotiate with the authorities, undergo health checks and other forms of personal control the women working in legal establishments have their identity as a prostitute reinforced and it becomes more of a 'career' as the working routines are formalised and essentialised (Raymond 2003). Legalisation can trap women in the sex industry and restrict, rather than increase, their choice about how they work and when they work and what type of services they are required to provide.

The suggestion that commercialising the sex trade will allow some women to work as independent professionals and to set up their own business and operate out of their own premises is a little myopic. Considerable difficulties in this respect have been reported in the Netherlands. Thus:

[But] in the wake of legalization and licensing, prostitutes too will have to comply with the new rules or pay the higher prices for licensed property and put their prices up. And they too will be priced out of the market. Moreover, the taxman may have no qualms in taking their money, but the banks are in no hurry to lend it to individual prostitutes or small brothel owners. In all likelihood, only the big brothel owners will still to be able to offer services at a reasonable price. Far from making prostitutes independent, legalization may well force them into regular paid employment with powerful employers.

(Brants 1998: 633)

Another form of legalisation is the zoning of street prostitution and creating 'toleration zones' where women can contact clients in an area which is protected and policed and normally located away from residential areas. Thus the attraction of developing these formal zones is the promise of removing street prostitution from residential areas where it causes most offence and simultaneously providing an ostensibly safe and controlled area in which women can meet clients.

The Netherlands, with its predisposition towards 'pragmatic tolerance', experimented with this form of zoning in the 1990s introducing 'tipple zones' into a number of cities including Rotterdam, Utrecht and Amsterdam. In each of these locations the zones have been managed and funded by the municipalities and have been policed by a specialist team of officers.

Despite the fact that early reports of the zones claimed that they had reduced the level of nuisance in some residential areas, they have, over the past few years, been systematically closed down. There are a number of reasons why these managed zones have been closed. One of the main reasons is the continued opposition from the members of the public as a result of television programmes depicting the lives of those who work in these locations:

There have been a number of TV documentaries about the zones that show the daily reality of the lives of people living in the margins of society. Although the zones offer women a relatively safe place to work, the circumstances of street sex work are far from ideal. The public is confronted with images of women who suffer from physical and psychological problems, images of women who have stories about rude and sometimes violent clients and images of women who, suffering from withdrawal, sell their services for very little money and taking risks concerning their health and safety. Being confronted with this reality some journalists and politicians pose the question whether this is something local government should facilitate.

(Van Doorninck and Campbell 2006: 71)

As Marieke van Doorninck and Rosie Campbell explain, the demise of the zones was due in part to overcrowding, particularly because of the growing number of migrant women who joined the ranks of street prostitutes in the 1990s. The level of public support for the zones has also decreased over time. There were also a number of women involved in street prostitution who did not want to work inside these zones because they were too remote and uncongenial, and as the zones became more overcrowded and competitive some of the women who had previously worked there decided to work in other areas. The checking of papers and the issuing of licences for women working in the zones also provided an incentive for some women to work elsewhere.

Despite the manifest failure of these experiments with zoning in the Netherlands it has not deterred certain local authorities in the UK from flirting with this option and considering the introduction of some form of 'managed zone' in their localities (Hubbard 1997). This is mainly because of the desire to respond to the pressures of local communities to remove street prostitution from residential areas in a number of urban centres in the UK, and at the same time create a space in which the women involved can be contained and supported.

There was until the late 1990s what was described as a 'non-harassment' zone in the Leith area of Edinburgh close to the docks. As this area was redeveloped and gentrified the incoming residents objected to the existence of a red light district and to the presence of prostitution on 'their' streets. Consequently the local authority sought to find an alternative location where the women could work, but because of objections from other residents, and the remoteness of alternative sites, no designated area could be found. Consequently, the local authority withdrew it's support for establishing a formally sanctioned zone in which those involved in street prostitution could operate (Edinburgh City Council 2003).

The experience of Edinburgh highlights the difficulties of moving from informally sanctioned red light districts in which street prostitution is to some extent tolerated, to the citing of formally designated areas that involves what is seen as the official sanctioning and endorsement of prostitution. In practice, in many urban centres in the UK, a compromise position has been adopted in which the police have developed strategies for moving women away from those residential areas where there are sustained objections and to other areas such as industrial areas or parks where there is less local opposition. However, because of issues of safety and isolation, women are generally uneasy about working in these areas and gravitate back to the more familiar and accessible residential areas where they feel more secure (Matthews 2005).

Interestingly in the UK, the rationale for constructing officially designated or legalised zones was that it offered a new approach to women, giving them more autonomy while normalising prostitution and enhancing rights. However, as Corbin (1990) has argued, various forms of spatial segregation have been used historically to render prostitution both accessible but invisible. The creation of an enclosed milieu in different urban centres is designed to limit moral and physical 'contamination' while ensuring that street prostitution remains under the supervision of the authorities. It is also interesting to note that historically male homosexual prostitution has not been subject to the same form of spatial controls.

The recent debate about the spatial control of street prostitution has been stimulated by the reconstruction of the postfordist city involving changing urban relations and social movements. It is no accident that in this changing configuration of space and attendant social sensibilities that finding a suitable location for the operation of street prostitution is becoming increasingly difficult. Those locations in which street prostitution has historically been allowed to operate are no longer able to accommodate this activity and those non-residential areas to which it is being redirected are unsafe, inaccessible and bad for business.

Prohibition

Prohibition or suppression involves the criminalisation of the exchange of sexual services for payment. Prohibition is normally associated with America and Sweden although there are considerable differences in the policy object-ives and public attitudes in both countries. In America virtually all states with the exception of Nevada criminalise the commercial exchange of sexual services:

> Every state in the United States defines the action of a person who offers or provides sex for money as a crime. Every state also makes it a crime to knowingly, with the expectation of monetary gain, encourage or compel a person to sell sex for money. Every state also makes it a crime to receive something of value, not for legal consideration, knowing that it was earned through the act of prostitution. Most states also impose criminal sanctions on the owners of properties where commercial sex takes place, and on people who reside in such places. In a few states the 'status' of being a prostitute is a crime. Some states make it a crime to buy sex.
>
> (Law 2000: 530)

Thus in most states of America both the women involved in prostitution and male clients are generally culpable. However, even where legal rules apply equally to buyers and sellers, law enforcement resources including undercover agents, are typically directed towards women rather than the men.

Because of the difficulties of generating evidence and mobilising witnesses the police often use entrapment methods. These methods have been the sub-ject of much criticism since they require the police officer to engage in the transaction and pretend to be a client offering money for sexual services before questioning and arresting the women. The difficulties and dangers of these methods of entrapment have led some communities in America to apply other legal and extra-legal methods of control such as publicity, impounding cars, revoking driving licences and requiring customers to attend 'John Schools'. There remain, however, problems of enforcement and compliance with customers resisting the imposition of these penalties. The main issue in

America is that despite the criminalisation of the selling and buying of sexual services, prostitution remains a prolific industry, and although some might argue that without the deterrent effect of criminalisation the numbers involved in prostitution would be even higher the high profile of prostitution in many American cities is widely seen as indication of the failure of prohibition.

The situation in Nevada is exceptional in America in that it is lawful to run licensed brothels, although prostitution remains illegal outside these establishments. It is estimated that in 1999 approximately 1,000 women worked in 33 licensed brothels in Nevada. Women have to register and submit to weekly health checks. Brothel owners impose additional requirements on the women charging them for rent, food, and normally take 50 per cent of their earnings (Farley 2007).

Sweden has taken a very different approach to prohibition. In Sweden, prostitution is regarded as a form of male violence against women and children. The aim in Sweden is to reduce or end prostitution rather than to manage it. Prostitution is seen to undermine gender equality. Legislation passed in 1999 made it a punishable offence to buy or attempt to purchase sexual services. The penalty is a fine or imprisonment for up to six months.

The unique nature of the Swedish form of prohibition is that unlike the United States of America it does not treat the women involved in prostitution and male clients as equally culpable. Instead, the women are seen largely as victims driven by poverty, drug addiction and forms of coercion while the male clients are seen as indulging their own fantasies and desires (Mansson 2001). Since the motivation and power relations between male clients and the women involved in prostitution are seen to be so different it makes little sense to treat them equally.

Since the introduction of the legislation prostitution has, according to official sources, decreased by 50 per cent and equally significantly, it has slowed down the rate of recruitment of young women into prostitution. It is also believed that the approach of criminalising male clients has deterred traffickers with the consequence that the number of women trafficked into Sweden is relatively low compared to neighbouring countries (Bindel and Kelly 2003). Opinion polls carried out since the legislation was adopted indicates that it has widespread support and one poll carried out in 2001 found that approximately 50 per cent of the population supports the new law. Between January 1999 and 2002 140 male 'punters' were convicted of purchasing sexual services.

Within the Swedish model there is a strong emphasis on developing exiting strategies and a recognition that these need to be well resourced and long-term. The decriminalisation of the women has resulted in them being able to access drug treatment programmes and other forms of support more easily. They also do not have to contend with the possibility of arrest by the police. Equally important is that their vulnerability is reduced. This in turn, no doubt, affects their level of victimisation. Since the new law was passed it is claimed by the agencies that have been developed to support those involved in prostitution, that the women contact them in greater numbers. It is also reported that there has been considerable successes in relation to exiting with 60 per cent of the 130 women who have been contacted between 2000 and 2003 leaving prostitution permanently (Ekberg 2004).

The position in Sweden is in opposition to the liberal position, which advocates a free market for the sex trade and the normalisation of prostitution. In Sweden, prostitution is seen as both harmful not only to those who engage in it, but also to society at large. In the name of gender equality the options of decriminalisation and legalisation are rejected on the grounds that these options, rather than address the issue of gender inequalities, perpetuate them. Thus:

> In Sweden, all forms of legal or policy measures that legalise different prostitution activities, such as brothels, or that decriminalise the perpetuators, including pimps, traffickers, brothel owners, and buyers, are seen by some as the most serious present day threats to gender equality and the rights of women and girls to live lives free of male violence. It is understood that the legalisation of prostitution will inevitably normalise an extreme form of sexual discrimination and violence and strengthen male dominance of all female human beings. Legalisation of prostitution means that the state imposes regulations with which they can control one class of women as prostituted.
>
> (Ekberg 2004: 1190)

The policy position in Sweden is not without its critics. Problems of enforcement remain, and there are claims that some of the women have moved from the street to off-street locations (Petterson and Tiby 2003). There are also some disgruntled women who remained working on these streets who claimed that the new law had deterred their prospective clients and made it harder to earn a living. It is also the case that the welfarism and support given to indigenous women is not extended by and large to 'trafficked' women who on arrest are only allowed to remain in Sweden to give evidence against their traffickers, after which they are normally deported (Svanstrom 2006).

There are also more jurisprudential concerns arising from the perceived asymmetrical nature of the law, since it forbids the buying of a service that is completely legal to sell. Liberal critics argue that it is wrong to criminalise male clients when they are engaged in transactions involving consenting adults where there is no indication of coercion. There are also issues of enforcing the law; it remains difficult to secure convictions against clients and some argue that criminalising the purchase of sexual services is more symbolic than practical. However, the enduring impact of the recently introduced legislation in Sweden is that it seems to have had a profound effect on social norms and social attitudes particularly amongst the male population who increasingly consider the purchase of sexual services as illegitimate.

Conclusion

It has been suggested that the main predictors of the level of prostitution in any country are likely to be the degree of social inequality and the nature of the dominant sexual ideology. However, in addition to these two determinants we must add the nature of public policy. In effect, whether prostitution is subject to regulationism, decriminalisation, legalisation or prohibition, this will influence the level of 'demand' and 'supply' significantly. These modes of regulation are therefore not simply responses to an existing phenomena but part of a strategy for constructing and shaping the phenomena itself. There is a symbiotic relationship between the form of prostitution and its control.

The evidence on the impact of the four major policy options – regulationism, legalisation, decriminalisation and prohibition – suggests that the most positive approaches include elements of regulationism, partial decriminalisation and the Swedish version of prohibition. Legalisation, as practiced in parts of Australia and the Netherlands, appears to be the least attractive option.

It has been suggested that neo-regulationism places the emphasis on limiting exploitation, protecting communities and addressing different forms of coercion and abuse. However, it remains, in the UK at least, tied to the 'stick and carrot' approach, which aims to combine protective measures with punitive responses. It does this in a way that continues to criminalise the women involved in the street trade while increasing their marginalisation and vulnerability. Partial decriminalisation, which involves the removal of sanctions against 'soliciting', appears to offer a way of reducing marginalisation and stigmatisation. As a result of the changing composition of those involved in street prostitution the removal of this legislation appears increasingly appropriate. The Swedish version of prohibition also fits well with partial decriminalisation and contributes to the objective of getting tough on kerb crawlers, pimps and those who exploit and abuse those involved in prostitution. By drawing these strands together it appears possible to develop a viable mode of regulation that could reduce the negative associations of prostitution while providing a more constructive and appropriate response for the women themselves.

Chapter 7

Regulating prostitution

Introduction

In this final chapter the aim is to outline a coherent and realistic policy response to prostitution. The main focus will be on street prostitution since this is the sector of prostitution which is considered to be most problematic, although some discussion of the off-street trade will also be entered into. These policy proposals are mainly directed to the situation in the UK, although it is anticipated that some elements of the proposed strategy will have relevance for other countries.

The starting point for developing a strategy in the UK is the recent government publications *Paying the Price* (2004) and *A Coordinated Prostitution Strategy* (2006). In these documents the government has laid out the basis of a reasonably clear and coherent response to prostitution. It is based on a fivefold strategy involving (a) the prevention of individuals, particularly young people, from becoming involved in prostitution; (b) tackling the demand for prostitution; (c) helping those involved in prostitution to exit; (d) sanctioning those who exploit or abuse women involved in prostitution and; (e) targeting commercial sexual exploitation and trafficking.

In developing this strategy the aim was to disrupt the street trade and reduce the number of women involved in street prostitution. The strategy involves a mix of enforcement and protection. The main rationale for reducing the level of street prostitution is to reduce disorder and to protect communities. There is a clear rejection in these documents of managed zones and large-scale legalisation. It is stated that:

> We reject the option of managed areas. The clear aim of Government will be to disrupt street sex markets and to significantly reduce the numbers involved in street prostitution. The focus of enforcement will be on kerb crawling to respond to community concerns and to reduce the demand for a sex market. We will bring forward reforms to the offence of loitering or soliciting to introduce a more rehabilitative approach and to remove the stigmatising term 'common prostitute'. Guidance will remain

firmly against the use of the criminal law in respect of children involved in prostitution save in the most exceptional circumstances – as a 'last resort' where services fail to engage with young people and they return repeatedly to the streets.

(Home Office 2006: 9)

The claim that prostitution is the 'oldest profession' and that it cannot be reduced in scale and impact is rejected. There is a clear belief that street prostitution should and can be significantly reduced. As with young people, adults who work on the streets and fail to engage with the available services will be subject to enforcement mainly in the form of anti-social behaviour legislation.

At the same time there is a token suggestion that two or three women should be allowed to work from the same premises without it being classed as a brothel. This would involve a modification of the exiting case law, which makes it illegal for two or more women to work together. It is noted, however, that the majority of women who work in London brothels are migrants, and that the market is becoming saturated, encouraging the use of unsafe sexual practices and probably increasing the level of exploitation in some sectors.

This stance remains essentially neo-regulationist and operates within the general framework set by Wolfenden, although with some significant amendments. The main concern is the visibility of prostitution and the sensibilities of affected communities. The approach is formally amoral but there is a clear sense that prostitution is not seen as a 'job like any other' and there is no suggestion that the sex industry should be allowed to operate freely. At the same time there is a focus on exploitation and abuse and the use of new legislation is advocated to prosecute those who engage in such practices. The underlying framework of this policy position was established in the mid 1990s by the All Party Parliamentary Group on Street Prostitution which signalled a shift in focus to protecting and decriminalising young people, prosecuting pimps, procurers and exploiters, together with a rejection of legalisation (Benson and Matthews 1996).

Paying the Price (2004) and *A Coordinated Prostitution Strategy* (2006) together with recent legislative changes provide a welcome contribution to policy formation and contain a number of positive elements. However, there remain a number of gaps and limitations in the strategy that need to be addressed. Some of these limitations are a function of the way in which policy is conceived. Other limitations are bound up with its implementation.

As might be expected, this neo-regulationist policy programme has attracted criticism from liberals and those advocating legalisation or total decriminalisation (UKNSWP 2004; ECP 2004; Boynton and Cusick 2006). These policy documents are first criticised for interfering with the market in prostitution by those who believe that the sex market should be allowed to operate uninterrupted. Relatedly, there is an objection to any attempt to reduce the street trade in order to protect communities. Third, some critics advocate a legalised on street or off-street system that endorses the sex trade and legitimises the activities of pimps, procurers and entrepreneurs. Others have objected to what they see as the 'stick and carrot' approach that involves providing incentives and welfare on the one hand and punitive policies on the other (Scoular and O'Neill 2007).

Some of these issues have been dealt with above, while others will be addressed in this chapter. Drawing on the evidence and arguments presented in earlier chapters of this book it is believed that the most appropriate strategies, which could be developed in the current context, include:

- Radically reducing the street trade in the short term and removing it in the long term;
- Further developing strategies to prevent young people becoming involved in prostitution;
- Decriminalising 'soliciting';
- Addressing the demand for sexual services;
- Promoting 'exiting' strategies;
- Intensifying the sanctions directed towards pimps, procurers and exploiters;
- Getting tough on all forms of violence and coercion directed towards prostitutes;
- Increasing the monitoring and surveillance of off street establishments.

Although this strategy can be seen as a radical form of neo-regulationism, the emphasis on the decriminalisation of soliciting, while providing intensive welfare support to those involved in street prostitution, gives the position an affinity with those who advocate partial decriminalisation as well as the Swedish form of prohibition.

The removal of street prostitution

It is suggested in the government publications that one of the key objectives is to achieve an overall reduction in street prostitution on the basis that 'street prostitution is not an activity we can tolerate in towns and cities'. However, the objective of reducing street prostitution is already being met. Figures from around the country indicate that the number of women engaged in street prostitution in a number of different urban centres is steadily declining (Matthews 2005). In some towns and cities in the UK, the number of women working on any one night is less than 10. These findings suggest that it may be possible to aim in the longer term, at least, for the removal of the street trade. The reasons for pursuing this more radical objective go beyond the need to protect communities and includes the need to protect the women who currently work on the streets as well as responding to the significant changes which are taking place in the use of space in the modern city.

It was evident from the events in Ipswich in 2006, where five women who were involved in street prostitution were murdered, that working on the streets is very precarious and that many of the women who expose themselves in this way are extremely vulnerable. The fact that some women in Ipswich kept on working after it became apparent that a murderer was targeting women involved in prostitution in the area was testimony to the desperation and vulnerability of these women (Addley 2006). But, however horrendous these murders were, they represent only the tip of a very large iceberg of violence directed towards women who work on the streets. Not surprisingly, following these murders the Crime and Disorder Reduction Partnership in Ipswich has moved away from a harm minimisation approach and instead has agreed on the objective of removing prostitution from the streets within five years (Ipswich 2007).

It has also been suggested above that the distinction in many cases between 'children' and 'adults' is less clear cut than it might appear since many of those who are over 18 and involved in prostitution began their involvement as children and therefore became involved in prostitution before they were deemed capable of making an informed choice. When the guidelines changed in the late 1990s in relation to how 'victims' under 18 should be dealt with the key principles included the development of an action plan to remove them from harm, investigate and identify those who have abused and exploited those concerned, mobilise a package of interventions including counselling, employment, housing and drug treatment and finally to develop a terminology which identifies the women concerned as 'victims' and those who exploit or coerce them as 'abusers, exploiters and coercers' (Brain 1998). This approach could be readily adapted to provide guidelines for developing an appropriate response to those over 18 working on the streets. Many of these women it has been suggested are more systematically victimised and more heavily addicted to drugs than those under 18. Besides the criteria of age the question of competence should also form part of the assessment regarding how women are treated.

It has been effectively demonstrated in the research and reviews of this issue that a holistic approach is necessary (Hester and Westmarland 2004; Hoigard and Finstad 1992). Such an approach needs to offer a user-friendly package, which is capable of addressing the various problems in a systemic rather than piecemeal way. The effectiveness of such an intensive welfare approach was ably demonstrated in the Malmo Project which sought to support women involved in prostitution, on the one hand, while assisting them to make more informed decisions, on the other. It is the presumption that, if such holistic packages are developed and implemented properly, the majority of those currently working on the street will sooner or later take advantage of them.

The Association of Chief Police Officers (ACPO) guidelines, however, include a provision to continue to prosecute the 'persistent and voluntary' return of young people to street prostitution. This, however, appears to be an inconsistent and unnecessary element of the policy. The minimal numbers of young people prosecuted in this way suggests that if an effective and well-resourced holistic, multi-agency, welfare-orientated approach is adopted then there should be no need for prosecutions. This is also likely to be the case for adults. In Sweden where the sale of sexual services was decriminalised in 1999 there has been a significant reduction in the street trade such that in Stockholm, for example, there are currently only a handful of women working on any one night (Hubbard et al. 2008).

At the same time there has been a substantial shift in the organisation and significance of space in urban centres over the past two decades or so. The reconstruction of the postfordist city has involved the radical reconfiguration of space and the divisions between 'public' and 'private' space have been transformed (Davis 1998; Sibley 1995). The regeneration of inner cities as well as gentrification in some areas has affected the distribution of populations and the movement of traffic. As a consequence the loosely established acceptance of red light districts has gradually broken down in many areas, and this has been accompanied by changing levels of public tolerance, particularly around issues of public order (Wilson and Kelling 1982). The mobilisation of local residents groups is, however, not just a function of spontaneously shifting levels of intolerance but of changing use and conceptions of space. It is no accident that so many residents' organisations drawn from different social and ethnic groups in different parts of the UK, as well as abroad, should respond in the way they have. Their mobilisation is in part a function of the changing nature of urban life in late modernity and the changing nature of space.

As the established areas of street prostitution become reorganised and increasingly contested the acceptability of street prostitution, as well as various other street-based activities including street drinking, vagrancy and begging, has decreased. The option to move street prostitution to non-residential locations such as industrial areas, wasteland or parks, which has been happening in some towns and cities, normally involves moving the street trade to relatively inaccessible and more dangerous locations. In many urban centres the 'natural habitat' of the street prostitute is in decline and there are limited available spaces which are safe, congenial and readily available to clients. Increasingly street prostitution appears anomalous and anachronistic. Consequently, attempts to mediate the ongoing tensions between residents groups and women working on the street is almost certainly doomed to failure (Scoular et al. 2007; Matthews 2007).

As Phil Hubbard (2004) has pointed out the 'cleansing of the Metropolis' is a feature of modern city life not only in cities like London but also in Paris and New York. In relation to improving the 'quality of life' for residents living and working in these locations there have been interventions in all of these locations to close down red light districts and remove forms of disorder which are seen to impede regeneration. This often involves the spatial relocation of prostitution:

> In short, isolating sex work within marginal and liminal urban locations does not serve to devalue commercial sex work; rather the opposite is true, with spatial marginalisation bringing sex work within the ambit of a *restricted economy* that hoards desire to commercial and capitalistic ends.
>
> (Hubbard 2004: 1699)

As the street trade becomes more marginalised and more problematic the commercialisation of the sex trade proceeds apace. New venues and sex clubs are becoming part of the new urban landscape, while different forms of prostitution are becoming established in traditional places of leisure and entertainment.

In sum, there are three main justifications for radically reducing the street trade in the short term and removing it in the longer term. These include the protection of communities, which have in many cases had their quality of life and freedom of movement limited for many years by the presence of street prostitution. Second, working on the streets is too dangerous and the women involved experience an unacceptable level of victimisation. The safety and well-being of these women requires that they are given every incentive to limit their exposure to victimisation. Third, the changing configuration of urban space means that existing red light districts are being transformed and the established sites for street prostitution are increasingly becoming contested. Alternative, non-residential sites tend to increase vulnerability and risk and make working on the street even more precarious.

Reducing the involvement and recruitment of those under 18

Over the last decade or so, a dramatic shift has taken place in how young people involved in prostitution are perceived and responded to. The transformation from 'offenders' to 'victims' represents a sea change in relation to policy and the depiction of this form of activity as 'child abuse' signals a change of public attitudes towards both young people and prostitution.

There can be little doubt that the change of categorisation from offenders to victims and the subsequent mobilisation of different support services and interventions has resulted in a substantial decrease in the number of young people entering and staying in prostitution in the UK. The limited acceptability of young people working on the streets has therefore had a depressing effect on recruitment. This, in turn, has contributed to the overall decrease in the number of women working on the streets and will almost certainly serve to decrease these numbers in the future.

However, there are other aspects of young peoples' involvement in prostitution which are not being addressed effectively. Child abuse and neglect, running away and being placed in local authority care have been identified as key pathways for entry into prostitution. Despite the fact that these routes into prostitution have been widely recognised for years, the available services remain conspicuously deficient.

The government's response has been to develop awareness in schools and to direct resources towards those deemed most 'at risk' of sexual exploitation. There is also a commitment in official circles to identify and support victims of sexual violence and child abuse. However, a recent Department of Health (2007) publication admitted that despite the potentially damaging effects of involvement in prostitution that 'awareness is low among mainstream health care practitioners about this issue' and that 'in too many cases victims and survivors are not identified and their support treatment and care needs are not met'.

Running away from home or from care has been repeatedly identified as increasing a young persons vulnerability to abusive adults. The provision for young runaways is grossly inadequate and there is an urgent need to provide suitable accommodation. Running away, being in local authority care, school exclusion, drug addiction, involvement in crime or being sent to prison serve to produce the marginalised groups from which those involved in street prostitution are predictably recruited. Where these groups have a history of child abuse the level of probability increases significantly.

Engaging in prostitution, however, can be a daunting experience. Usually young people are introduced to prostitution by either peers, pimps or procurers. Despite the array of government bodies, experts, publications and specialist groups who focus on protecting vulnerable children, prosecutions for procuring offences in England and Wales have decreased significantly over the last decade.

In sum, the situation of young people involved in prostitution has improved dramatically with the identification of those under 18 as victims of abuse. However, despite the rhetoric and chest thumping the level of action against facilitators, abusers and exploiters has been disappointing. One suspects that if the young people concerned came predominantly from well off middle class families rather than being disadvantaged 'throwaways', the response would be very different.

Decriminalising 'soliciting'

One of the few points of agreement between liberal and radical feminists in recent years has been the need to decriminalise soliciting-related offences. The arguments from both camps have a different emphasis but in general it is suggested that women engaged in street prostitution are driven by need, poverty, or a drug habit and are therefore less culpable. It is also argued that the women involved in prostitution are victims of patriarchal gender relations involving a double standard of morality. In addition it is argued that a significant percentage have been coerced, duped or deceived into becoming involved in prostitution, while others claim that the law on soliciting is discriminatory, ineffective or counterproductive.

The main obstacle to these continued calls for the decriminalisation of soliciting has been the issue of general deterrence and the concern by governments that such a step might be interpreted as an acceptance of women's involvement in prostitution. In relation to the argument concerning the deterrent effect of legislation and the possible effects that it might have on the women who are 'at risk' of entering prostitution such arguments had a certain credibility 20 years ago (Matthews 1986a; 1992). However, the composition and nature of street prostitution has changed over the past two decades, and as has been suggested above, we have moved from a position in which the majority of women involved in prostitution are motivated primarily by economic pressures to one in which the majority of those who currently work on the streets of the UK are drug addicted, damaged and desperate. For these women the laws on soliciting are likely to have little deterrent effect.

At the same time, if our aim is to radically reduce or remove street prostitution, it needs to be recognised that the criminalisation of soliciting significantly increases the vulnerability of those involved to both clients and pimps. It also reinforces their marginalisation. It is the quasi-legal status of these women and the sense of impunity that it engenders among those who aim to use and abuse them that accounts for much of the victimisation that they suffer. There is a symbiotic relationship between vulnerability and the infliction of violence and abuse. Thus the way to reduce violence against those involved in prostitution is not so much through the development of 'ugly mugs' campaigns and the like but by significantly reducing their vulnerability. Removing these criminal labels is a first step to giving women the power and authority to report abuse and coercion and to believe that such reports will be taken seriously and acted upon.

It has been suggested that those involved in street prostitution are better seen as victims than offenders. In the same way that the involvement of young people in prostitution has come to be seen as a form of child abuse, the involvement of those over 18 should be seen in similar terms. This is not only because many of those aged 18 and over began their involvement in prostitution while they were children but also because the victimisation they experience is both extensive and continuous. While exposed to this range of victimisation their chances of making informed decisions and constructive choices about their lives is limited. Our aim should be to increase choice and encourage agency.

If our objective is to remove or radically reduce street prostitution a decision has to be made whether we want to essentially increase the welfare response or extend the criminal justice response. While these may not necessarily be exclusive oppositions we can see that the type of response, which has been effective in dealing with young people, has involved a minimal amount of formal legal controls. Clearly, if forms of welfare intervention are developed which can reduce women's' motivation to engage in prostitution, address their personal social and economic needs, the need for criminal sanctions should be removed.

Decriminalisation of soliciting, however, does not mean a cessation of regulation. On the contrary, it suggests that we need to develop more imaginative and appropriate forms of intervention to deal with issues of disorder and to protect vulnerable communities. There are a range of measures in place for dealing with various forms of disorder and street prostitution that would fall within the category. Such measures do not involve the mobilisation of legal sanctions but rather the application of more informal measures instigated by other agencies than the police. These can involve spatial strategies including road management schemes and community campaigns, together with various forms of monitoring and surveillance.

Policing prostitution

The police response to prostitution has historically been equivocal. Policing prostitution has generally been seen as a low priority in police work and the police response has largely been a function of community and political pressure. During much of the twentieth century one of the main interests that the police had in prostitution was using the women as sources of information. Even the establishment of specialist Vice Squads in the 1970s and 1980s did little to increase the priority of prostitution but rather relegated it to a specialist and relatively autonomous area of work. Working in, or managing, a vice squad has never been a fast track to promotion.

It was the result of considerable pressure from local communities living in or around red light districts that forced the police in the 1980s to take the issue more seriously. In some areas, the development of multi-agency initiatives proved effective in reducing the level of street prostitution. However, most police initiatives have either been short lived, sporadic or poorly resourced. In many cases, however, the aim has not so much been to remove street prostitution but to keep 'a lid on it' and to construct a 'manageable problem'. The focus has mainly been on the street trade and although brothels increased in numbers during the 1980s and 1990s, the police in many parts of the country turned a blind eye to their operation, and only took action when there was a disturbance or on incident, or where there were reports of underage or trafficked women working in the establishments (Benson and Matthews 2000).

The police response in recent years has changed as the issue of prostitution has moved up the social and political agenda. However, the National Policing Plan in England and Wales has no specific objectives or targets relating to prostitution, which is significant as the police are increasingly being driven by targets. A recent report by the Association of Chief Police Officers (Brain et al. 2004) notes that 'Police forces in England and Wales are currently operating in a policy vacuum: the law regarding prostitution is clear, but the application of the law – in order to best serve the public and protect the vulnerable – is not'. The police are, however, working more closely with other agencies. In doing so, they have moved away from an enforcement approach (except in relation to kerb crawlers) and towards a more informal role increasingly referring the women involved in street prostitution to support agencies (Matthews 2005).

However, the shift away from enforcement and the downsizing and dissolution of a number of Vice Squads has not resulted in a significant shift of police attention to the growing off-street trade. Although there have been a few noticeable interventions aimed at brothels using trafficked women or underage girls, there has been no noticeable redirection of resources towards the off-street trade or towards procurers or exploiters. In fact the cynical view of recent changes towards a multi-agency approach is that the police in many areas have relinquished a degree of responsibility and de-prioritised this issue, while reverting to the relatively low key stance which was evident in the 1970s and early 1980s.

One strategy for dealing with the street prostitution is to resort to the use of Anti-Social Behaviour Orders (ASBOs). This option has been suggested by ACPO as a 'last resort'. There is evidence that in different parts of the country that this civil sanction is becoming the preferred way of responding to those women who are seen not to respond to other interventions (Matthews 2005). The use of ASBOs has however been met with considerable controversy not only in relation to prostitution but also in relation to the other forms of anti-social behaviour for which they have been used (Solanki et al. 2006: Squires and Stephen 2005).

While ASBOs may seem an appropriate measure of 'last resort' in dealing with persistent problems of anti-social behaviour, and fit will within the multi-agency approach favoured by the government, there are a number of problems in issuing ASBOs to women involved in street prostitution. It has been suggested, for example, that rather than being a sanction of 'last resort' they are deployed as a 'quick fix' and that rather than being used when welfare sanctions have been exhausted they are used instead of welfare options (Sagar 2007). Particularly when ASBOs are given on conviction (CRASBOs) the usual welfare and case conferencing approach can be bypassed with the 'offender' being given a 'double sanction', since the conditions of the CRASBO are added on to the existing punishment. ASBOs in general do very little to address the causes of women's involvement in prostitution or provide much in the way of rehabilitation (May and Hunter 2004). They also normally involve a spatial component, which includes a strategy of deliberate displacement potentially moving the problem from one area to another. Most importantly, the issuing of an ASBO is likely to be detrimental to an exiting strategy as the women may be forced to move to an area where they are unknown and the necessary supports and resources are unavailable (Matthews et al. 2007).

If we see women involved in street prostitution mainly as victims rather than offenders the use of ASBOs becomes largely inappropriate for this group. A well-resourced and strategically implemented holistic welfare package would be the most effective and appropriate mode of intervention. If an ASBO is to be used in relation to this issue in order to deal with public order concerns, then kerb crawlers would seem to be a more appropriate target, since the threat of exclusion and shaming which is normally attached to these orders would almost certainly have a major deterrent effect on this group – particularly the use of ASBOs on conviction.

In relation to women involved in street prostitution the most appropriate role for the police is to act primarily as a referral agency, directing women to the relevant agencies and welfare programmes. The use of Drug Treatment and Testing Orders (DTTO) have been shown to have some benefits in terms of reducing drug use and improving physical and psychological health, although there have been problems with implementation (May et al. 2001).

In short, there is a need to move away from the adoption of the familiar 'stick and carrot' or enforcement plus support approach in relation to women involved in street prostitution that is currently being advocated by the government (Home Office 2004). The time and effort saved by no longer arresting and prosecuting the women working on the streets could be spent addressing issues of abuse, exploitation, and the monitoring of the off-street trade, as well as increasing the focus on kerb crawling.

Addressing demand

The focus of attention has moved towards kerb crawlers over the past decade. Increasingly they have become identified as the main offenders in relation to public order offences, often driving around residential areas in significant numbers or approaching women on the street. It has become recognised that the motivation of kerb crawlers and street prostitutes is very different and that the aim of regulation should not be to treat both parties in the same way.

It has also been the case that much kerb crawling is more opportunistic than once believed and that a significant number of men are more interested in observing in voyeuristic fashion the women on the street, than actually paying for sexual services. In a similar way, it has become evident that many of these 'punters' are relatively easily deterred. Once cautioned or arrested the vast majority are deterred and never re-arrested (Brewer et al. 2006). There is convincing evidence that if the objective is to remove street prostitution then focusing interventions on kerb crawlers is both legitimate and effective.

Over the past decade or so a wide range of sanctions and strategies have been developed to catch or deter kerb crawlers. They include fines, shaming, the use of CCTV and car number plate recognition systems, police patrols and observation as well as the endorsement of driving licences. In some areas forms of entrapment have been used whereby women police officers stand on the streets and when they are approached by kerb crawlers the men are cautioned or arrested (Matthews 1993; Westmarland 2006). The available evidence suggests that fines have a limited deterrent effect on kerb crawlers and that shaming strategies are more effective as a specific deterrent.

In Sweden, where the purchase of sexual services has been criminalised, there has been a significant decrease in street prostitution and a lower level of trafficking than in neighbouring countries. Importantly, the recent law which makes the purchase of sexual services illegal appears to have affected public attitudes in general with the majority of teenage men seeing the purchase of sexual services as illegitimate. It is still the case, however, that in most countries around the world the purchase of sexual services is seen as a right. However, there are issues about the role of male clients and there have been attempts recently to 'responsibilise' punters by encouraging them to report brothels that are suspected of using trafficked women in both the Netherlands and the UK. This move towards 'responsibilisation' could be extended by making clients who purchase the service of trafficked women culpable in the same way as purchasing the sexual services of those under 16 is punishable. This could act as both a specific and general deterrent to clients and may help to reduce the level of trafficking.

Another option that has been tried has been kerb crawler's re-education programmes or 'John Schools' as they are known in America and Canada. These are diversion projects that are offered to kerb crawlers as an alternative to being charged or going to court. This diversion programme is based on the view that the kerb crawler is the principle offender. These programmes tend to embrace a number of objectives including rehabilitation and education. They normally involve a short course outlining the effects of kerb crawling for which the kerb crawlers are required to pay.

Some beneficial effects have been reported in relation to the men who have attended these courses, with some men expressing the view that their attitude towards prostitution and the women involved in it had changed. However, the overall evaluation of these programmes suggests that their effectiveness is limited (Campbell and Storr 2001). One programme which was run in West Yorkshire in 1998–99, for example, found that less than 50 per cent of kerb crawlers arrested in the area ended up on the programme and some concern was expressed about the ability of the programme to change perceptions and attitudes in such a short period. The authors of the evaluation of the West Yorkshire pilot scheme concluded that: 'It was felt that the programme was effective in challenging gender stereotypes', but suggested that 'follow-up work would be needed to reinforce the learning of the day' (Hanmer and Bindel 2000). One interesting finding from this report was that 60 per cent of the men were married or co-habiting, 30 per cent were single and only 8 per cent were divorced or separated.

Similar results have been reported in evaluations of 'John Schools' in Canada. The Canadian programme was found to be highly selective and that while it was claimed that the courses were mainly educational it was found that they tended to be extremely moralising and designed to blame and shame the kerb crawlers (Fischer et al. 2002; Wahab 2006). It was also reported that half of the men on the programme did not feel that they had committed a crime and had only engaged in the programme in order to avoid a criminal record.

Focusing sanctions on male kerb crawlers, however, is not to suggest that prostitution is any more 'demand driven' than 'supply led' (Raymond 2004). Prostitution, in its various forms, is the product of a complex set of dynamics including social and economic inequalities, gender differences and sexual ideologies as well as the playing out of differential power relations.

There is evidence, however, that the visibility and availability of sex markets encourages demand and heightens awareness by providing a stimulus to potential clients. Removing street prostitution from residential areas will therefore be likely to reduce the number of men motivated to pay for sexual services (Cameron 2004). As noted above a study of male clients conducted in Canada found that one in four reported that it was a spontaneous decision while just over 40 per cent said that it was the availability and visibility of prostitutes that had motivated them (Lowman and Atchinson 2006).

However, the observation that prostitution cannot be reduced to 'demand' for sexual services does not mean that this exonerates the client. Because the 'demand' may be more opportunistic than is normally assumed does not reduce the culpability of those who pay for sex as Julia O'Connell-Davidson (2005) has argued. She claims that we have a myopic vision of those under 18 as being innocent and pure and these stereotypes cast children as passive, removing agency from these young people who in many cases, she argues, enter prostitution because it is preferable to poverty or in some cases, starvation. In criticising feminist abolitionists, on the one hand, who see the demand for commercial sex as the driving force behind prostitution and liberal 'sex work' feminists, on the other, who fail to examine clients in any detail because they want to normalise prostitution and treat it as just another form of employment she argues that: 'calls for strong and punitive legal responses to those who pay minors for sex are rather less progressive then they may initially appear' (p. 110).

Her argument is based on the claim that all those paying for sex with minors are not necessarily paedophiles while, sex tourism, paid or unpaid, is much more common than might be assumed. Many of these clients who pay for the sexual services of minors she informs us also come from 'bleak and impoverished backgrounds' while those, for example, who work in the gold mines of South Africa would otherwise be condemned to months of sexual abstinence. In other settings, she suggests, men who do not engage in prostitution use might be labelled 'gay' or 'unmanly' and these possible depictions, we are told, may have 'very serious consequences for the individual involved' (p. 122).

These rationalisations for normalising, and not penalising, the purchase of sexual services from minors by adult males culminates in the following statement:

> Consider, for example, the fact that there are places in the world where it is estimated that between 15 and 30 per cent of those working in prostitution are under the age of 18 and that up to 75 per cent of the male population engage or have engaged in prostitution use. In such places, proposals to penalise anyone who buys sex from a minor could translate into proposals to incarcerate more than half of the male populations. Calls for the universal application of harsh penalties against those who buy sex from children do not necessarily represent either a realistic or a humane response to the problem.
>
> (O'Connell Davidson 2005: 122)

Thus, in a series of untenable propositions that ultimately fail to transcend opposition between abolitionist and liberal feminisms O'Connell Davidson, who in a previous publication appeared to come down on the side of the former, now sides with the latter (O'Connell Davidson 1998). All sense of culpability and exploitation is reduced and this ostensibly radical critique ends up by defending the status quo. The assertion that we need to deal with world poverty before we can address issues of prostitution produces a rationalisation of the current situation in which 'child abuse', as many international bodies prefer to refer to child prostitution, is allowed to continue unregulated.

If we take O'Connell Davidson's arguments to their logical conclusion, it would follow that being apart from wives and partners for any period of time, being abroad on holiday or business, or not wanting to be seen by one's peers as being gay or unmanly, provides sufficient justification for purchasing the services of poor and desperate children. The claim that we should refrain from punishing adult male clients because in some countries so many have used those under 18 for sexual gratification is weak and disingenuous, as is the suggestion that incarceration is the only and most likely sanction. Imagine a parallel argument that suggested that we should refrain from punishing the perpetrators of domestic violence because it is so prevalent, or because offenders are poor and deprived, or because not to hit women might be considered to be unmanly.

The normalisation of the purchase of sexual services of minors by adult males, which O'Connell Davidson advocates, even goes beyond the position that most starry-eyed liberals would advocate. Indeed, the apology that she offers for male use of minors goes far beyond the usual liberal rationalisations which try to justify male demand in terms of imperious sexual urges or the loneliness and frustration of single men.

Exiting

The number of women who would like to leave street prostitution is probably much greater than we realise. At the same time it is widely acknowledged that the majority of those involved in street prostitution will need considerable help and support to overcome the various impediments they face. The chaotic lifestyle, drug dependency, homelessness, mental and physical health problems as well as the difficulty of finding alternative, well-paid employment are reoccurring obstacles to exiting.

In the last few years, however, support and specialist groups in different countries have been developing forms of intervention to help women exit. To date, these interventions have produced mixed results. In some cases this is because of a lack of funding, in others it is because the exiting strategy adopted is not structured in a way that is able to help women overcome the obstacles they face. Evaluations of these exiting projects suggest that if they are to be effective they need to be structured, comprehensive, integrated, individually tailored and in some cases interventions will need to be long-term. There is a distinction between 'exiting' and 'stopping' and these terms refer to the time since the person was last involved in prostitution, recognising that in many cases that there may be reversals.

One of the central tensions in relation to exiting is that there is considerable ambivalence amongst the relevant support agencies regarding the significance of helping women to leave prostitution. Consequently, many agencies adopt a largely reactive approach and in some cases offer a piecemeal response which may involve addressing one particular issue such as drug addiction without offering a comprehensive package. Many of the agencies involved remain dedicated to a harm reduction approach (Rekart 2005). Although this approach has provided a useful vehicle for providing much needed resources to marginalised groups in the past, there is a danger that by failing to address the underlying social, economic and political issues, that harm reduction becomes a self-sustaining regulatory mechanism and a form of governance which props up prostitution and perpetuates harms rather than addressing the material base of these harms. Thus in relation to drug treatment it has been argued that:

> What we see developing in the official harm-reduction programmes and policies certainly offers needed comfort for the immediate problems of individuals trapped in addiction. There is no question of its practical and needed effectiveness at the levels of individual and population health.

But without a return to the more socially and politically active analysis it began with, harm reduction offers little prospect for real, long-term solutions to the increasing difficulty posed to society by drug use. Harm reduction has 'matured' into a conservative movement, an apology for the past and an effective means to carry that historic dysfunction into the future (Roe 2005: 248).

Just as the harm reduction approach to drug use has resulted in the creation of a manageable form of addiction so there is a real danger that the harm reduction model applied to prostitution could create a manageable but ageing cohort of prostitutes whose identity and purpose is to organise and regulate itself according to that classification.

There is therefore a need to move beyond piecemeal reactive and short-term approaches and develop a more proactive strategy that is in line with available 'best practice'. This will involve the development of more specialist agencies that can provide well-funded and well-structured flexible packages. As the numbers on the streets decline, and as the services which have been put in place over the last few years flourish, the development of effective exiting strategies must be equally if not more cost-effective than recycling these women through the criminal justice system.

Pimping, procuring and exploitation

One of the main tenets of *Paying the Price* (2004) and related government publications is the commitment to get tough on those who coerce, groom, abuse and exploit women involved in prostitution. Despite the welcome commitment of these proposals, its actual implementation involves a loud bark but small bite.

Paying the Price suggests that those abused and controlled through prostitution should be protected and that those measures directed at the sexual exploitation of both adults and children should be rigorously enforced. The available figures, however, show that between 1990 and 2000 the number of cautions and convictions issued for procuring in magistrates' courts in England and Wales decreased from 444 to 58. The introduction of the Sexual Offences Act 2003 was designed to deal with issues of child prostitution, trafficking and exploitation. The legislation introduced a number of new offences. However, between 2003–04 and 2006–07 the number of prosecutions for the 'Exploitation of Prostitution' remained fairly stable at around 85 recorded offences, while 'Abduction of Female' fell from 403 to 21 over the same period. It is too early to tell whether this new legislation will make a significant impact on these type of offences, but offences like 'Sexual activity involving a child under 16' and 'Sexual Grooming' are being recorded more often which may be a result of a growing focus on these issues.

The problem in terms of intervention is gathering evidence and one response to that has been the greater use of surveillance. Witness support is available for those under 17 in England and Wales and video links are available for child witnesses in cases involving violence, kidnapping and abduction. The strategy suggested by *Paying the Price* to address the exploitation of adults involved in prostitution by pimps and brothel keepers is, however, conspicuously thin.

The issue that arises is whether the Sexual Offences Act 2003 provides the conceptual framework or practical components that will allow the government to achieve its stated objectives. The different elements of the legislation focus on the process of 'recruiting controlling and facilitating' the involvement of young people in prostitution. This division of the various roles, which can be played in relation to the involvement of people in prostitution, is an important step. It has been emphasised above that the process of facilitation is a key element in the process of recruitment into prostitution and this process applies as much to peers, family and friends as it does to pimps and procurers. It might be useful, however, to add a fourth dimension to this approach and penalise those who stop or impede those who wish to leave prostitution.

The key element in these processes is gaining evidence. This is one of the reasons why the decriminalisation of soliciting has been advocated. The removal of this legal sanction should allow those involved in prostitution to more freely report those who groom or coerce them. The removal of the legal sanction should also serve to decrease the vulnerability of the women and thereby reduce the sense of impunity that some perpetrators feel they have. The greater autonomy and independence resulting from the decriminalisation of soliciting will therefore make the women concerned less attractive targets for those who wish to abuse/coerce or exploit them while increasing the confidence and independence of the women concerned.

There have been significant difficulties in gaining convictions for 'living off immoral earnings'. If the person is more of a partner than a pimp, or they are supplied with drugs rather than money, or if they have other legitimate sources of income, proving the case can be difficult. The sanction is maintained more as a deterrent to those who might otherwise use or exploit women involved in prostitution, but in terms of gaining convictions it has a limited effectiveness.

There is a clause in the Sexual Offences Act 2003, which relates to the inciting of those with mental illness to engage in commercial sexual activity. This clause could usefully be extended to all those who lack the competence or capacity to make reasonable choices about their involvement in prostitution and this would include those, for example, whose level and style of drug use significantly impedes their judgement. The enactment of such a clause in any future legislation could make a major impact on the scale of street prostitution.

The Sexual Offences Act 2003 has also brought in new legislation on brothels and it is now an offence for 'a person to keep or manage, or act to assist in the management of a brothel to which people resort for practices involving prostitution'. Given that most 'massage parlours' and 'saunas' in the UK are brothels the enforcement of this legislation could potentially close down most, if not all, of these establishments. The limited deployment of this legislation, however, reflects the ambivalence of the authorities who are charged with its implementation: namely the police and local authorities. There are also some recent provisions to review the licensing of these establishments. A more effective way of controlling exploitation and abuse in the sex industry may be through the seizure of assets. The Proceeds of Crime Act 2002 made it possible to seize the assets of suspected offenders. This is a potentially a useful weapon for effectively limiting the activities of unscrupulous entrepreneurs, particularly those who use underage girls or engage in coercive exploitative practices. In general the aim should be, as far as possible, to limit third party involvement and control in prostitution.

Thus, although the Sexual Offences Act 2003 represents a positive set of proposals its implementation, to date, remains limited. The problem is overcoming the ambivalence and lack of commitment of the key agencies. There is a clear objective of extending protection to children but the protection offered to adults is limited. Moreover, sexual grooming itself is not made an offence and there remain problems of demonstrating proof, gathering evidence and showing intent (Ost 2004).

Stopping traffic?

There is generally no accepted definition of trafficking and no single unitary act which can be identified as representing trafficking. 'Trafficking' therefore remains an umbrella term to cover a number of different processes including the recruitment, transportation and control of persons. Even if we differentiate trafficking from smuggling and focus on the processes of sexual exploitation the variations on the practices and policies involved make it difficult to define 'trafficking persons' with any precision. Also the focus on the more extreme cases of abduction, and the forced migration of women into prostitution has promoted the 'white slave' myth and deflected attention from the more mundane and routine ways in which women travel from one country to another and end up in prostitution. While there can be little doubt that the sex industry has fed off women's economic marginalisation in many underdeveloped countries there are ongoing unresolved debates about the extent to which these women were forced or moved voluntarily. In cases where womens' involvement is seen to be voluntary the response is often punitive and exclusionary.

In recent years, however, a more victim-centred approach has developed in Europe in response to many social issues. However, in relation to foreign women involved in prostitution they only tend to receive protection and support if they cooperate with the authorities, provide information or testify against traffickers. They are not generally seen as worthy victims and indeed are often depicted as being complicit in their own exploitation. Being recognised as victims, as Jo Goodey (2004) has argued, is an important condition for receiving rights and privileges. Although countries like the UK call for a 'victim-centred' approach to prostitution, victims of trafficking do not normally receive much help (D'Cunha 2002). Indeed, they often experience 'secondary victimisation' and they are not routinely offered protection and support unless they testify against traffickers.

The UN Declaration of Basic Principles of Justice for Victims of Crime and Abuse of Power (1985) promised a broad based response to victims, which involved providing information, care and respect, protection, restitution and compensation. Although this and the subsequent Convention Against Transnational Organised Crime (2000) provide some useful guidelines at the international level on how victims of trafficking should be treated there remain problems of compliance:

> [However] 18 years after the 1985 UN Declaration and Council of Europe Recommendation, there remains a great deal of non-compliance at the level of the individual member states. In this regard EU member states have to rethink their victim-centred policy in line with the latest Commission Directive Against Trafficking to accommodate trafficking victims within the framework of a renewed criminal justice response to victims of crime in general. This means a rethinking of policy to engage with a new set of victims who because of their status as illegal immigrants and prostitutes associated with organised criminal gangs, do not fit the stereotype of the 'deserving victim'.
>
> (Goodey 2004: 42)

At best, foreign women involved in prostitution tend to be treated as second-class victims. Many writers and policy makers have pointed out the complexities of distinguishing between 'voluntary' and 'forced' trafficking, but few have provided a clear, precise and legally enforceable distinction that might work in practice. If our aim is to promote the human rights of trafficked women and provide support then we need to work through this opposition (Monro 2006). The coercion/consent dichotomy does not capture the ways in which the majority of migrant women become involved in prostitution. For thousands of poor women who find work either in the sex trade or elsewhere, it would be impossible without some form of facilitation (Kelly 2003). Although the UN Optional Protocol of Trafficking in Human Beings, known widely as the Palermo Agreement, attempts to move beyond the coercion/consent dichotomy and includes notions of debt bondage and deception, few of the countries that have signed up to the convention (including the UK) have translated it into national law. Consequently, we need to look not only at how women enter the sex industry but also the contexts and conditions within which they work. In cases in which the working conditions experienced by trafficked women would not be accepted in any other sphere of employment objections should be voiced.

Jo Goodey has also suggested that action taken against traffickers should not predominantly rely on the evidence given by trafficked women. Instead she argues more consideration should be given to the seizing of criminal assets and laundered money through police intelligence and fraud investigations. Recent national legislation and the European Convention Against International Organised Crime (2000) should make it easier for states to pursue traffickers through alternative means that do not necessarily require witness testimonies.

Overcoming dualisms

It is becoming increasingly recognised that the debate around prostitution is getting bogged down in a series of dichotomies (victim/agent; coercion/consent, etc), with the result that it tends to oscillate between oppositions and extremes. Two major groups have been established. On one side, 'sex work' liberals want to normalise prostitution, and see it as just another form of employment which, however demeaning, is seen as being no better or worse than many other forms of service work which disadvantaged women engage in. The abolitionists and radical feminists, on the other side, claim that prostitution is a distinctively different form of activity than other types of service work and has damaging personal and social consequences.

Although at one level there is a fundamental political and conceptual difference between these two positions the debate is fuelled by drawing freely on selected myths or drawing selected examples from a very differentiated sex industry. Thus, while it has been argued in line with the radical feminists that prostitution is not a 'job like any other', the liberal feminists are correct to point out that within this differentiated industry those working off street engage in a form of work which in some cases is less like slavery and more like free wage labour. However, the challenge which arises for 'sex work' liberals who emphasise 'choice' and 'agency' is to identify how choice is structured for different women and, in particular, where the competence and freedom of individuals is such that they cannot exercise a reasonable or acceptable level of choice. For example, in line with other forms of 'legitimate' work which would not engage problematic drug users or those who were forced by their 'partners' to work, liberals need to take a clear stance and direct such individuals away from prostitution. In the same way those that see, or want to see, prostitution as a 'job like any other' need to work to eradicate those forms of coercion, grooming and deception which are used to engage women in prostitution, and at the same time organise to remove all of the slave-like conditions associated with the sex industry.

Some 'sex work' liberals have, as we have seen, advocated that those working in the sex industry should have decent conditions of employment. However, as has become evident in the Netherlands, where entrepreneurs are required to provide decent conditions of employment, it has led to the demise of the legalised sex industry, since these entrepreneurs are not particularly interested in respecting these standards. It is also the case that if the sex industry provides proper conditions of work, security of employment, sick leave, holidays, pension schemes and the like, the wages paid would probably come to resemble those paid in other service sectors, supermarkets and fast food outlets. In this situation, the majority of these women would almost certainly change prostitution for waitressing, or other 'legitimate' forms of service work.

As for the discussion of victim-agency it has been suggested that this opposition is in many cases false and that victims are also agents, and that their agency is in part conditioned by their experience of victimisation. Victimisation can be a consequence of agency or a spur to agency. By the same token, agency is not 'free' in some absolute sense but signals that individuals are always engaged in action and that such action is more or less consciously directed within the material constraints in which individuals necessarily operate.

Overcoming the structure/agency dualism as has been suggested is difficult. This dichotomy runs through social science and remains an unresolved tension in much of the literature. It has been suggested, however, that 'pathways' analyses goes some way to resolving this opposition since it take some account of structure while acknowledging the role of the agency. It is not the case, however, that this book adequately resolves these long standing dualisms but it emphasised that the reality of the decision-making process, the experience and the situation of those who are caught up in the prostitution business, takes place within the large grey area which is located somewhere between these various oppositions. A realistic policy has to begin by exploring the evidence from the mundane and routine rather than the extremes (Benson and Matthews 1995). In this way we can generate evidence-based policy rather than provide policy driven evidence.

Conclusion

In this book the aim has been to examine the evidence and arguments on prostitution in order to develop a coherent analysis and policy position. At the same time it has been the intention to try to work through some of the dualisms which have hindered the development of constructive policies and practices. In doing so, the intention has been to steer a path between 'sex work' liberals and their conservative opponents.

There is a danger, of course, in being too prescriptive. More cautious writers prefer to be more suggestive and less directive in the policy arena, as they are aware that situations can change quickly and that policy proposals which sound very sensible at one moment can in a short period of time become outdated. The danger of laying out a policy programme in any detail is that it gives the opportunity to critics to pick up on minor points rather than to assess the overall direction of suggested change. The current policy direction in the UK is positive but it is overly cautious and does not go far enough. The speed of implementation has also been slow.

The murders in Ipswich in 2006 marked a turning point in public and political opinion and brought into question liberal policies centred around harm reduction and normalisation. Something more radical and proactive, however, is required and pressure needs to be placed on the authorities to implement some of the more positive elements of its current programme, while simultaneously encouraging policy makers to introduce some more radical and far-reaching reforms.

Bibliography

Acton, W. (1857) *Prostitution Considered in Its Moral, Social and Sanitary Aspects in London and Other Large Cities With Proposals for the Mitigation and Prevention of Its Attendant Evil.* London.

Addley, E. (2006) 'Murder Victim Had Spoken of Fear on the Streets'. *The Guardian* 13 December.

Agustin, L. (2006) 'The Conundrum of Women's Agency: Migration and the Sex Industry' in R. Campbell and M. O'Neill (eds.) *Sex Work Now.* Collumpton: Willan.

Allwood, G. (2004) 'Prostitution Debates in France' in *Contemporary Politics,* vol. 10, No. 2: 145–57.

Anderson, B. and O'Connell-Davidson, J. (2003) *Is Trafficking in Human Beings Demand Driven? A Multi-Country Pilot Study.* Geneva: International Organisation for Migration.

Audet, E. and Carrier, M. (2006) 'Green Lights for Pimps and Johns'. Sisyphe. http://sisyphe.org/article.php3?id.article=2230.

Ayre, P. and Barrett, D. (2000) 'Young People and Prostitution: An End to the Beginning?' in *Children and Society,* vol. 14: 18–59.

Bagley, C. and Young, L. (1987) 'Juvenile Prostitution and Child Sexual Abuse; A Controlled Study'. *Canadian Journal of Community and Mental Health* vol. 6: 5–26.

Bailey, J. (2002) *Conversations in a Brothel.* Hodder/Headline.

Banach, L. and Metzenrath, S. (2000) *Principles for Model Sex Industry Legislation.* Sydney: Scarlet Alliance.

Barr, R. and Pease, K. (1990) 'Crime Displacement and Placement' in M. Tonry and N. Morris (eds.) *Crime and Justice,* vol. 12: University of Chicago Press.

Barry, K. (1979) *Female Sexual Slavery.* Englewood Cliffs NJ: Prentice Hall.

Barry, K. (1995) *The Prostitution of Sexuality.* New York University Press.

Barry, K. (1998) 'Female Sexual Slavery: The Problem', Policies and Cause For Feminist Action' in E. Beneparth and E. Stoker (eds.), *Women, Power and Policy: Toward the Year 2000.* Pergamon Press.

Barthes, R. (1973) *Mythologies.* St. Albans: Paladin.

Bauman, Z. (1998) 'On Postmodern Uses of Sex', *Theory, Culture and Society,* vol. 15, No. 3: 19–33.

Benoit, C. and Millar, A. (2001) *Dispelling Myths and Understanding Realities:*

Working Conditions, Health Status and Exiting Experiences of Sex Workers. Victoria, Canada: Prostitutes Empowerment, Education and Resource Society.

Benson, C. and Matthews, R. (1995) 'Street Prostitution: Ten Facts in Search of a Policy' in *International Journal of Sociology of Law*, vol. 23: 395–415.

Benson, S. and Matthews, R. (1996) *Report to the Parliamentary Group on Prostitution.* London: Middlesex University.

Benson, S. and Matthews, R. (2000) 'Police and Prostitution: Vice Squads in Britain' in R. Weitzer (ed.), *Sex for Sale.* London: Routledge.

Bernstein, E. (2001) 'The Meaning of the Purchase: Desire Demand and the Commerce of Sex', *Ethnography* vol. 2, No. 3: 389–420.

Bindel, J. (2006) *No Escape? An Investigation into London's Service Provision for Women Involved in the Commercial Sex Industry.* London: The Poppy Project.

Bindel, J. and Kelly, L. (2003) *A Critical Examination of Responses to Prostitution in Four Countries: Victoria, Australia; Ireland; the Netherlands; and Sweden.* London: London Metropolitan University.

Bindman, J. and Doezema, J. (1997) *Redefining Prostitution as Sex Work in the International Agenda.* Anti-Slavery International www.walnet.org/csis/papers/redefining.html

Bird, J. (2006) *A Rolls Royce Service for the Homeless Please.* The Big Issue Manifesto. London.

Bourgois, P. (2002) 'Crack and the Political Economy of Social Suffering' in *Addiction Research and Theory*, vol. 11, No. 1: 31–7.

Boynton, P. (1998) *Somebody's Daughter, Somebody's Sister: A Reflection of Wolverhampton Working Women's Lives.* Aston Business School.

Boynton, P. and Cusick, L. (2006) 'Sex Workers to Pay the Price' *British Medical Journal.* January: 190–1.

Bradford, M. (2005) *Developing Exit Strategies for Female Outdoor Sex Workers in Barnet, Enfield and Haringey.* London: Sexual Health on Call (SHOC).

Brain, T., Davis, T. and Phillips, J. (2004) *Policing Prostitution: ACPOs Policy, Strategy and Operational Guidelines for Dealing with Exploitation and Abuse Through Prostitution.* Association of Chief Police Officers.

Brants, C. (1998) 'The Fine Art of Regulated Tolerance: Prostitution in Amsterdam' in *Journal of Law and Society*, vol. 25, No. 4: 621–35.

Brewer, D., Potterat, J., Muth, S., Roberts, J. (2006) 'A Large Specific Deterrent Effect of Arrest for Patronizing a Prostitute', *PLUS ONE* (1): e60.d01: 10. 1371/journal.pone.0000060

Brewis, J. and Linstead, S. (2000) *Sex, Work and Sex Work: Eroticising Organisations.* London: Routledge.

Brewis, J. and Linstead, S. (2000) 'The Worst Thing is the Screwing (2): Context and Career in Sex Work', *Gender, Work and Organisation*, vol. 7, No. 3: 168–81.

Bristow, E. (1977) *Vice and Vigilance: Purity Movements in Europe Since 1700, Dublin.* Gill and Macmillan.

Brock, D. (1998) *Making Work, Making Trouble: Prostitution as a Social Problem.* Toronto: University of Toronto Press.

Brooks-Gordon, B. and Gelsthorpe, L. (2003) 'What Men Say When Apprehended for Kerb Crawling: A Model of Prostitutes' Clients Talk', *Psychology, Crime and Law*, vol. 9, No. 2: 145–71.

Boyle, S. (1994) *Working Girls and Their Men.* London: Smith Gryphon Publishers.

Brown, A. and Barrett, D. (2002) *Child Prostitution and Child Sexual Abuse in Twentieth Century England*. Collumpton: Willan.

Buchanan, J. (2004) 'Missing Links? Problem Drug Use and Social Exclusion' in *Probation Journal*, vol. 51, No. 4: 387–97.

Burnett, R. and Maruna, S. (2004) 'So "Prison Works" Does It? The Criminal Careers of 130 Men Released from Prison Under Home Secretary Michael Howard', *The Howard Journal* vol 43, No. 4: 390–404.

Busby, K., Downe, P., Gorkoff, K., Nixon, K., Tutty, L. and Urset, J. (2002) *Examination of Innovative Programming for Children and Youth Involved in Prostitution*. Simon Fraser University, Vancouver: The Fresa Centre for Research on Violence Against Women and Children.

Cameron, S. (2004) 'Space, Risk and Opportunity: The Evolution of Paid Sex Markets', *Urban Studies*, vol. 41, No. 9: 1643–57.

Campbell, R. (2002) *Working on the Street: An Evaluation of the Lynx Project 1998–2001*. Liverpool: Hope University.

Campbell, R. and O'Neill, M. (2006) *Sex Work Now*. Collumpton: Willan.

Campbell, R. and Storr, M. (2001) 'Challenging the Kerb Crawler Rehabilitation Programme', *Feminist Review* No. 67. Spring: 94–108.

Chapkis, W. (1997) *Live Sex Acts: Women Performing Erotic Labour*. London: Cassell.

Christie, N. (1986) 'The Ideal Victim:' in E. Fattah (ed.), *From Crime Policy to Victim Policy*. London: Macmillan.

Chudakov, B., Han, K., Belmaker, H. and Cwikel, K. (2002) 'The Motivation and Mental Health of Sex Workers', *Journal of Sex and Marriage Therapy*, vol. 28: 305–15.

Church, S., Henderson M., Barnard M. and Hart, K (2001) 'Violence by Clients Towards Female Prostitutes in Different Work Settings', *British Medical Journal* 332: 524–5.

Classen, C., Palesh, O., Aggarwal, R. (2005) 'Sexual Revictimisation: A review of the Empirical Literature', *Trauma, Violence and Abuse*, vol. 6, No. 2: 103–29.

Corbin, A. (1990) *Women for Hire: Prostitution and Sexuality in France after 1850*. Cambridge, Mass: Harvard University Press.

Cowan, R. (2006) 'Men Urged to Report Brothels Using Trafficked Women'. *The Guardian*, February 22.

Coy, M., Horrath, L. and Kelly, L. (2007) *Its Just Like Going to the Supermarket: Men Buying Sex in East London*. London: London Metropolitan University.

Cusick, L. and Hickman, M. (2005) 'Trapping in Drug Use and Sex Work Careers', *Drugs, Education, Prevention and Policy*, vol. 12, No. 5: 369–79.

Cusick, L., Martin, A., May, T. (2003) *Vulnerability and Involvement in Drug Use and Sex Work*, Home Office Research Study 268. London: Home Office.

Dalla, R. (2000) 'Exposing the Pretty Woman Myth', *Journal of Sex Research*, vol. 37: 344–53.

Dalla, R. (2002) 'Night Moves: A Qualitative Investigation into Street Level Sex Work', *Psychology of Women Quarterly*, vol. 26: 63–73.

Dalla, R., Xia, Y., Kennedy, H. (2003) 'You Just Give Them What They Want and Pray They Don't Kill You', *Violence Against Women*, vol. 9, No. 11: 1367–94.

Darrow, W. (1990) 'Prostitution, Intravenous Drug Use and HIV in the United States' in M. Plant (ed.), *Aids, Drugs and Prostitution*. London: Routledge.

Davenport, J. (2001) 'Slave Trade in Vice Girls'. *Evening Standard*, December 16.

Davis, M. (1998) *City of Quartz: Excavating the Future of Los Angeles*. London: Pimlico.

Davis, N. (2000) 'From Victims to Survivors: Working with Recovering Street Prostitutes' in R. Weitzer (ed.), *Sex for Sale*. London: Routledge.

Davis, S. and Shaffer, M. (1994) *Prostitution in Canada: The Invisible Menace or the Menace of Invisibility?* http://www.walnet.org/csis/papers/sdavis.html

Dawson, P. and Cuppleditch, L. (2007) *Impact Assessment of the Prolific and Priority Offender Programme*. Online report 08/07. London: Home Office.

D'Cunha, J. (2002) *Trafficking in Persons: A Gender and Rights Perspective*. New York: United Nations.

Denning, A. (1993) *The Profumo Affair* (2nd edn). London: Pimlico.

Department of Health (2001) *National Plan for Safeguarding Children From Commercial Exploitation*. London: DOH.

Department of Health (2007) *New NHS Guidelines to Support Victims of Abuse*. London: DOH.

Devlin, P. (1965) *The Enforcement of Morals*. Oxford: Oxford University Press.

Dickson, S. (2004) *Sex in the City: Mapping Commercial Sex Across London*. London: The Poppy Project.

Ditton, J., Farrell, S., Bannister, J., Gilchrist, W. and Pease, K., (1999) 'Reactions to Victimisation: Why has Anger Been Ignored?', *Crime Prevention and Community Safety: An International Journal* vol. 1: 37–53.

Doezema, J. (1998) 'Forced to Choose: Beyond the Voluntary vs Forced Prostitution Dichotomy' in K. Kempadoo and J. Doezema (eds.), *Global Sex Workers: Rights, Resistance, and Redefinition*. New York: Routledge.

Doezema, J. (2000) 'Loose Women or Lost Women: The Re-emergence of the Myth of White Slavery in Contemporary Discourses on Trafficking in Women', *Gender Issues*, vol. 18, No. 1: 38–54.

Doezema, J. (2002) 'Who Gets to Choose? Coercion, Consent and the UN Trafficking Protocol', *Gender and Development*, vol. 10, No. 1: 20–7.

Dunn, V. (1984) *A Study of Prostitution in Finsbury Park*. North London Polytechnic.

Economist (2004) 'It's a Foreigner's Game'. *The Economist*, vol. 372, Issue 8391, September 4.

Edinburgh City Council (2003) *Prostitution in the Leith Area*. November. Report No. CEC/95/0304/H & SW.

Ekberg, G. (2004) 'The Swedish Law That Prohibits the Purchase of Sexual Services' *Violence Against Women*, vol. 10, No. 10: 1187–218.

Ekos (2005) *Value for Money, Review and Team Development*. Glasgow: Ekos.

Engels, F. (1972) *The Origin of the Family, Private Property and the State*. New York: Pathfinder Press.

English Collective of Prostitutes (1997) 'Campaigning for Legal Change' in G. Scambler and A. Scambler (eds), *Rethinking Prostitution*. London: Routledge.

English Collective of Prostitutes (2004) *Criminalisation: The Price Women and Children Pay*. London: English Collective of Prostitutes.

Ennew, J., Gopal, K., Heeran, J., Montgomery, H. (1996) *Children and Prostitution: A Literature Review and Annotated Bibliography*. New York: UNICEF.

Ericsson, L. (1980) 'Charges Against Prostitution: An Attempt at a Philosophical Assessment', *Ethics* vol. 90: 355–6. Reprinted in R. Matthews and M. O'Neill (eds), *Prostitution*. Ashgate.

Farrington, D. (1992) 'Explaining the Beginning of Progress and the End of Anti-Social Behaviour From Birth to Adulthood' in J. McCord (ed.), *Facts, Frameworks and Forecasts*. New Brunswick: Transaction Books.

Faugier, J. and Sargeant, M. (1997) 'Boyfriends, Pimps and Clients' in G. Scambler and A. Scambler (eds.), *Rethinking Prostitution*. London: Routledge.

Farley, M. (2004) 'Bad for the Body, Bad for the Heart: Prostitution Harms Women Even if Legalised or Decriminalised', *Violence Against Women*, vol. 10, No. 10: 1087–125.

Farley, H. (2007) *Prostitution and Trafficking in Nevada: Making the Connections*. San Francisco, CA: Prostitution Research and Education.

Farley, M. and Barkan, H. (1998) 'Prostitution, Violence and Stress Disorder', *Women and Health*, vol. 27, No. 3: 37–49.

Farley, M. and Kelly, V. (2000) 'Prostitution: A Critical Review of the Medical and Social Science Literature', *Women and Criminal Justice*, vol. 11, No. 4: 29–64.

Farrell, G. and Pease K. (1993) *Once Bitten, Twice Bitten: Repeat Victimisation and Its Implications for Crime Prevention*, Crime Prevention Unit Paper 46. London: Home Office.

Farrell, S. (2005) 'On the Existential Aspects of Desistance From Crime' vol. 28, No. 3: 367–86.

France, A. and Homel, R. (2006) 'Societal Access Routes and Developmental Pathways: Putting Social Structure and Young Peoples Voice Into the Analysis of Pathways Into and Out of Crime', *The Australian Journal of Criminology*, vol. 39, No.3: 295–309.

Fischer, B., Wortley, S., Webster. C., Kirst, M. (2002) 'The Socio-Legal Dynamics and Implications of "Diversion": The Case of the Toronto "John School" Diversion Programme for Prostitution Offenders', *Criminal Justice*, vol. 2, No. 4: 385–410.

Flowers, R. (2001) *Runaway Kids and Teenage Prostitution: Americas Lost, Abandoned and Exploited Children*. Westport Connecticut: Praeger.

Foucault, M. (1985) *The Use of Pleasure: The History of Sexuality*, vol. 2. London: Penguin.

Giddens, A. (1979) *Central Problems in Social Theory*. London: Palgrave/Macmillan.

Giddens, A. (1992) *On the Transformation of Intimacy*. Cambridge: Polity Press.

Giobbe, E. (1993) 'An Analysis of Individual, Institutional and Cultural Pimping', *Michigan Journal of Gender and Law* vol. 4: 33–57.

GLADA (2004) *An Evidence Base for the London Crack Cocaine Strategy*. London: Greater London Drug and Alcohol Alliance.

Goodey, J. (2003) 'Migration Crime and Victimhood: Responses to Sex Trafficking in the EU', *Punishment and Society*, vol. 5, No. 4: 415–31.

Goodey, J. (2004) 'Sex Trafficking in Women From Central and Eastern European Countries: Promoting a Victim Centred and Women Centred Approach', *Feminist Review*, vol. 76: 26–45.

Gossop, M., Powis, B., Griffiths, P. and Strang, J. (1995) 'Female Prostitutes in South London: Use of Heroin, Cocaine and Alcohol and Their Relationship to Health Risk Behaviours', *AIDS Care*, vol. 7, No. 3: 253–60.

Green, J. (1992) *Its No Game: Responding to the Needs of Young People at Risk or Involved in Prostitution*. Leicester: National Youth Agency.

Green, J., Mulroy, S., and O'Neill, M. (1997) 'Young People and Prostitution; From a

Youth Service Perspective' in D. Barrett (ed.), *Child Prostitution in Britain*. London: The Children's Society.

Hagan, J. and McCarthy, B. (1997) *Mean Streets: Youth Crime and Homelessness*. Cambridge: Cambridge University Press.

Hall, S. (1980) 'Reformism and the Legislation of Consent' in National Deviancy Conference (ed.), *Permissiveness and Control*. London: Macmillan.

Hanmer, J. and Bindel, J. (2000) *Report of the Kerb Crawler Re-Education Programme*. Leeds: Leeds Metropolitan University.

Harding, L. (2006) 'Kidnapped at Ten and Held for Eight Years: The Girl in the Cellar'. *The Guardian*, August 25.

Harper, Z., and Scott, S. (2006) *Meeting the Needs of Sexually Exploited Young People in London*. London: Barnardo's.

Hart, H. (1962) *Law, Liberty and Morality*. Oxford: Oxford University Press.

Hedin, U-C. and Mansson, S-V. (2000) 'The Importance of Supportive Relationships Among Women Leaving Prostitution' in M. Farley (ed.), *Prostitution, Trafficking and Traumatic Stress*. New York: The Haworth Press.

Herman, J. (1992) *Trauma and Recovery*. Basic Books.

Hester, H. and Westmarland, N. (2004) *Tackling Street Prostitution: Towards a Holistic Approach*, Research Study 279. London: Home Office.

Hoigard, H. and Finstad, L. (1992) *Backstreets: Prostitution, Money and Love*. Cambridge: Polity Press.

Home Office (2004) *Paying the Price: A Consultation Paper on Prostitution*. London: Home Office.

Home Office (2006) *A Coordinated Prostitution Strategy and a Summary of Responses to Paying the Price*. London: Home Office.

Hubbard, P. (1997) 'Red Light Districts and Toleration Zones: Geographies of Street Prostitution in England and Wales', *Area* vol. 29, No. 2: 129–40.

Hubbard, P. (1998) 'Community Action and Displacement of Street Prostitution: Evidence from British Cities', *Geoforum*, vol. 29, No. 3: 269–86.

Hubbard, P. (2004) 'Cleansing the Metropolis: Sex work and the Politics of Zero Tolerance', *Urban Studies*, vol. 41, No. 9: 1687–702.

Hubbard, P., Matthews, R. and Scoular, J. (2008) 'Re-Regulating Sex Work in the EU: Prostitute Women and the New Spaces of Exception'. Gender Place Culture (forthcoming).

Hubbard, P. and Saunders, T. (2003) 'Making Space for Sex Work: Female Street Prostitution and the Production of Urban Space', *International Journal of Urban and Regional Research*, vol. 27, No. 1: 75–89.

Hunter, G. and May, T. (2004) *Solutions and Strategies: Drug Problems and Street Markets*. London: Home Office.

Hunter, S. (1994) 'Prostitution is Cruelty and Abuse to Women and Children', *Michigan Journal of Gender and Law*, vol. 1: 1–14.

Ipswich Crime and Disorder Reduction Partnership (2007) *Ipswich Street Prostitution Strategy 2007–2012*.

Jaget, C. (1980) *Prostitutes: Our Life*. Bristol: Falling Wall Press.

Jeffreys, S. (1997) *The Idea of Prostitution*, Melbourne: Spinifex Press.

Jeffreys, S. (1999) 'Global Sexual Exploitation: Sex Tourism and the Traffic in Women', *Leisure Studies*, vol. 18, No. 3: 179–96.

Jeffreys, S. (2000) 'Challenging the Adult Child Distinction in Theory and Practice on Prostitution', *International Journal of Feminist Politics*, vol 2, No. 3: 359–79.

Jeffreys, S. (2004) 'The Legalisation of Prostitution: A Failed Experiment' online at www.sisyphe.org.

Jenness, V. (1990) 'From Sex as Sin to Sex as work: COYOTE and the Reorganization of Prostitution as a Social Problem', *Social Problems*, vol. 37: 403–20.

Jordan, J. (2005) *The Sex Industry in New Zealand: A Literature Review*. Wellington: New Zealand: Ministry of Justice.

Kantola, J. and Squires, J. (2004) 'Discourses Surrounding Prostitution Policies in the UK' in *Women's Studies*, vol. 11: 77–101.

Karras, R. (1996) *Common Women: Prostitution and Sexuality in Medieval England*. New York: Oxford University Press.

Katz, J. (1991) 'The Motivation of Persistent Robbers' in M. Tonry (ed.), *Crime and Justice*, vol. 14. Chicago: University of Chicago Press.

Kempadoo, K. and Doezema, J (1998) *Global Sex Workers: Rights, Resistance and Redefinition*. New York: Routledge.

Kesler, K. (2002) 'Is a Feminist Stance on Prostitution Possible? An Exploration of Current Trends' in *Sexualities*, vol. 5, No. 2: 219–35.

Kelly, L. (2003) 'The Wrong Debate: Reflections on Why Force is Not the Key Issue With Respect to Trafficking in Women for Sexual Exploitation', *Feminist Review*, 73: 139–44.

Kelly, L. and Regan, L. (2003) *Stopping Traffic: Exploring the Extent of, and Responses to, Trafficking in Women for Sexual Exploitation in the UK*, Policy Research Series Paper 125. London: Home Office.

Kilvington, J., Day, S., and Ward, H. (2001) 'Prostitution in European Policy', *Feminist Review*, No. 67: 78–92.

Kinnell, H. (2006) 'Murder Made Easy: The Final Solution to Prostitution' in R. Campbell and M. O'Neill (eds.), *Sex Work Now*. Collumpton: Willan.

Kirby, P. (1995) *Word From the Street: Young People Who Leave Care and Become Homeless*. London: Centerpoint/Community Care/Reed Business Publishing.

Law, S. (2000) 'Commercial Sex: Beyond Decriminalisation', *Southern Californian Law Review*, vol. 73: 523–610.

Lean, M. (2003) 'The Red Lights Go Green in Birmingham' *www.forachange.co.uk*.

Lee, M. and O'Brien, R. (1995) *The Game's Up*. London: The Children's Society.

Leigh, C. (1997) 'Inventing Sex Work' in J. Nagle (ed.), *Whores and Other Feminists*. New York: Routledge.

Levy, A. (2004) *Stigmatised, Marginalised and Criminalised: An Overview of the Issues Relating to Young People and Children Involved in Prostitution*. London: NSPCCP.

Lewis, S., Maguire, M. Raynor, P. Vanstone, M. and Vennard, J. (2003) *The Resettlement of Short-Term Prisoners; An Evaluation of Seven Pathfinder Programmes*. Findings 200. London: Home Office.

Lim, L. (1998) *The Sex Sector: The Economic and Social Basis of Prostitution in South East Asia*. Geneva: ILO.

London Assembly (2005) *Street Prostitution in London*. London Safer Committee: Greater London Authority.

Lopes, A. (2006) 'Sex Workers and the Labour Market' in R. Campbell and M. O'Neill (eds.), *Sex Work Now*. Collumpton: Willan.

Lowman, J. (1987) 'Taking Young Prostitution Seriously' *Canadian Review of Sociology and Anthropology*, vol. 24, No. 1: 99–116.

Lowman, J. (1992) 'Street Prostitution Control: Some Canadian Reflections on the Finsbury Park Experience' *British Journal of Criminology*, vol. 32, No. 1: 1–17.

Lowman, J. and Atchinson, C. (2006) 'Men Who Buy Sex: A Survey in the Greater Vancouver Regional District', *Canadian Review of Sociology and Anthropology*, vol. 43, No. 3: 281–96.

Malarek, V. (2004) *The Natashas: The New Global Sex Trade*. London: Vision.

Mansson, S-V. (2001) 'Men's Practices in Prostitution: The Case of Sweden' in B. Pease and K. Pringle (eds), *A Man's World? Changing Men's Practices in a Globalized World*. London: Zed Books.

Mansson, S-V. and Hedin, U-C. (1999) 'Breaking the Matthew Effect – On Women Leaving Prostitution', *British Journal of Social Welfare*, 8: 67–77.

Maruna, S. (2000) *Making Good: How Ex-Convicts Reform and Rebuild their Lives*. Washington: American Psychological Association.

Matthews, R. (1986) 'Beyond Wolfenden: Prostitution, Politics and the Law' in R. Matthews and J. Young (eds), *Confronting Crime*. London: Sage.

Matthews, R. (1986a) *Policing Prostitution: A Multi-Agency Approach*. Paper 1. Centre for Criminology, Middlesex University.

Matthews, R. (1992) 'Developing More Effective Strategies for Curbing Prostitution' in R. Clarke (ed.), *Situational Crime Prevention: Successful Case Studies*. New York: Harrow and Heston.

Matthews, R. (1992) 'Regulating Street Prostitution and Kerb Crawling; A Reply to John Lowman. *British Journal of Criminology* vol. 32, No. 1: 18–22.

Matthews, R. (1993) *Kerb Crawling, Prostitution and Multi-Agency Policing*. Crime Prevention Unit Series Paper 43. London: Home Office.

Matthews, R. (1997) *Prostitution in London: An Audit*. Centre for Criminology: Middlesex University.

Matthews, R. (2005) 'Policing Prostitution: Ten Years On', *British Journal of Criminology*, vol. 45: 1–20.

Matthews, R (2007) 'The Prostitution Strategy: A Response', *Community Safety Journal*, vol. 6, Issue 3: 4–6.

Matthews, R., Easton, H., Briggs, D. and Pease, K. (2007) *Assessing Anti-Social Behaviour Orders*. Bristol: Policy Press.

Matthews, R. and Pitts, J. (2001) 'Beyond Criminology' in R. Matthews and J. Pitts (eds.), *Crime, Disorder and Community Safety*. London: Routledge.

Matthews, R. and Young, J. (1992) 'Reflections on Realism' in R. Matthews and J. Young (eds.), *Rethinking Criminology: The Realist Debate*. London: Sage.

Matza, D. (1964) *Delinquency and Drift*. John Wiley and Sons.

May, T., Edmunds, M. and Hough, M. (1999) *Street Business: The Links Between Sex Markets and Drug Markets*. London: Home Office.

May, T., Harocopos, A. and Hough, M. (2000) *For Love or Money: Pimps and the Management of Sex Work*. Policy Research Series Paper 13. London: Home Office.

May, T., Harocopos, A. and Turnbull, P. (2001) *Selling Sex in the City*, Social Science Research Paper 14. London: South Bank University.

May, T. and Hunter, G. (2006) 'Sex Work and the Problem of Drug Use in the UK: The Links, Problems, and Possible Solutions' in R. Campbell and M. O'Neill (eds), *Sex Work Now*. Collumpton: Willan.

McClanahan, H., McClelland, G., Abram, K. and Teplin, L. (1999) 'Pathways Into Prostitution Among Female Jail Detainees and Their Implications for Mental Health Services' in *Psychiatric Services*, vol. 50, No. 12: 1606–13.

McConnell, K. (2006) *A Girl Called Karen: A True Story of Sexual Abuse and Resilience*. London: John Blake Publishing.

McIntosh, M. (1978) 'Who Needs Prostitutes? The Ideology of Male Sexual Needs'. in C. Smart and B. Smart (eds.), *Women, Sexuality and Social Control*. London: Routledge and Kegan Paul.

McKeganey, N. (2005) 'Street Prostitution in Scotland: The Views of Working Women', *Drugs, Education, Prevention and Policy*, vol. 13, No. 2: 151–66.

McKeganey, N. (2006) 'The Lure and the Loss of Harm Reduction in UK Drug Policy and Practice' *Addiction Research and Theory*, vol. 14, Issue 6: 557–88.

McKeganey, N. and Barnard, M. (1996) *Sex Work on the Streets: Prostitutes and their Clients*. Buckingham: Open University Press.

McLeod, E. (1982) *Working Women: Prostitution Now*. London: Croom Helm.

Meier, R. and Geis, G. (1997) *Victimless Crime? Prostitution, Drugs, Homosexuality, Abortion*. Los Angeles: Roxbury Publishing Company.

Melrose, M. (2004) 'Of Tricks and other Things: An Overview' in M. Melrose and D. Barrett (2004), *Anchors in Floating Lives: Interventions with Young People Sexually Abused Through Prostitution*. Lyme Regis: Russell House.

Melrose, M. (2007) 'The Government's New Prostitution Strategy: A Cheap Fix for Drug-Using Sex Workers?', *Community Safety Journal*, vol. 6, No. 1: 18–27.

Miller, P. (2001) 'A Critical Review of Harm Minimisation Ideology in Australia' *Critical Public Health*, vol. 11: 167–78.

Miriam, K. (2005) 'Stopping the Traffic in Women: Power, Agency, and the Abolition of Feminist Debates over Sex-Trafficking', *Journal of Social Philosophy*, vol. 36, No. 1: 1–17.

Moffitt, T. (1994) 'Natural Histories of Delinquency' in G. Weitzcamp and H. Kerner (eds.), *Cross National Longtitudinal Research on Human Development and Criminal Behaviour*. Dordrecht: Kluwer.

Monro, V. (2006) 'Stopping Traffic? A Comparative Study of the Responses to the Trafficking in Women for Prostitution', *British Journal of Criminology*, vol. 46, No. 2: 334–56.

Monto, M. (2000) 'Why Men Seek Out Prostitutes' in R. Weitzer (ed.), *Sex For Sale*. New York: Routledge.

Monto, M. (2004) 'Female Prostitution, Customers and Violence, in *Violence Against Women*, vol. 10, No. 2: 160–88.

Nadon, S., Koverola, C. and Schindlemann, E. (1998) 'Antecedents to Prostitution: Childhood Victimisation', *Journal of Interpersonal Violence*, vol. 13: 206–97.

Nagle, J (1997) *Whores and Other Feminists*. New York: Routledge.

Nash, R., Futton, M., Keetley, K. and Cusick, L. (2004) *Hackney, Haringey and Islington: Rapid Assessment and Responses on Sex Work and Problematic Drug Use*. London: Centre for Research on Drugs and Health Behaviour, Imperial College.

Newburn, T. (1992) *Permission and Regulation: Law and Morals in Post-War Britain*. London: Routledge.

O'Connell Davidson, J. (1998) *Prostitution, Power and Freedom*. Cambridge: Polity Press.

O'Connell Davidson, J. (2002) 'The Rights and Wrongs of Prostitution', *Hypatia*, vol. 7, No. 2: 84–98.

O'Connell Davidson, J. (2005) *Children in the Global Sex Trade*. Cambridge: Polity Press.

O'Connell Davidson, J. (2006) 'Will the Real Sex Slave Stand Up?'. *Feminist Review*, 83: 4–22.

O'Malley, P. (2004) *Risk, Uncertainty and Government*. London: Glasshouse Press.

O'Malley, P. (2006) 'Risk and Restorative Justice: Governing Through the Democratic Minimisation of Harms' in I. Aertson, T. Daems and L. Robert (eds.), *Institutionalizing Restorative Justice*. Collumpton: Willan.

O'Neill, M. (1997) 'Prostitute Women Now' in G. Scambler and A. Scambler (eds.), *Rethinking Prostitution*. London: Routledge.

O'Neill, M. (2001) *Prostitution and Feminism: Towards a Politics of Feeling*. Cambridge: Polity Press.

O'Neill, M. and Campbell, R. (2004) *Walsall Prostitution Consultation Research: A Participatory Action Research Project*. Walsall South Health Action Zone.

O'Neill, M. and Campbell, R. (2006) 'Street Sex Work and Local Communities' in R. Campbell and M. O'Neill (eds), *Sex Work Now*. Collumpton: Willan.

Ost, S. (2004) 'Getting to Grips with Sexual Grooming', *Journal of Social Welfare and Family Law*, vol. 26, No. 2: 147–59.

Outshoorn, J. (2004) *The Politics of Prostitution: Women's Movements, Democratic States and the Globalisation of Sex Commerce*. Cambridge University Press.

Outshoorn, J. (2005) 'The Political Debates on Prostitution and Trafficking of Women', *Social Politics*, vol. 12, No. 1: 141–55.

Overall, C. (1992) 'What's Wrong With Prostitution?', *Signs*. vol. 17, No. 4.

Palmer, T. and Stacey, L. (2002) *Stolen Childhood*. London: Barnardo's.

Parent-Duchalet, A. (1836) *De la Prostitution dans la Ville de Paris* (2 vols). Paris: J. B. Bailliere.

Parker, H., Aldridge, J. and Measham, F. (1998) *Illegal Leisure: The Normalisation of Adolescent Recreational Drug Use*. London: Routledge.

Pateman, C. (1991) 'What's Wrong with Prostitution?' in C. Pateman (ed.), *The Sexual Contract*. Cambridge: Polity Press.

Pearce, J., Williams, M., Galvin, C. (2002) *It's Someone Taking a Part of You: A Study of Young Women and Sexual Exploitation*. London: National Children's Bureau.

Pearl, J. (1987) 'The Highest Paying Customers: America's Cities and the Costs of Prostitution Control', *Hastings Law Journal*, vol. 38, No. 4: 769–800.

Pease, K. (2008) 'Victims and Victimisation' in S. Soham, O. Beck and M. Kett (eds.), *International Handbook of Penology and Criminal Justice*. Boca Raton, FL: CRC Press.

Penfold, C., Hunter, G., Campbell, R. and Barnham, L. (2004) 'Tackling Client Violence in Street Prostitution: Inter-agency Working Between Outreach Agencies and the Police', *Policing and Society*, vol. 14, No. 4: 365–79.

Pettersson, T. and Tiby, E. (2003) 'The Production and Reproduction of Prostitution' *Journal of Scandinavian Studies in Criminology and Crime Prevention*, vol. 3: 154–72.

Phoenix, J. (1999) *Making Sense of Prostitution*. Houndmills Basingstoke: Macmillan.

Phoenix, J. (2000) 'Prostitute Identities: Men, Money and Violence', *British Journal of Criminology*, vol. 40, 37–55.

Phoenix, J. (2002) 'In the Name of Protection: Youth Prostitution Policy in England and Wales', *Critical Social Policy*, vol. 22, No. 2: 353–75.

Phoenix, J. and Oerton, S. (2005) *Illicit and Illegal: Regulation and Social Control*. Collumpton: Willan.

Pitcher, J. and Aris, S. (2003) *Women and Street Sex Work: Issues Arising from an Evaluation of an Arrest Referral Scheme*. Research Briefing 7. London: NACRO.

Pitts, M., Smith, A., Grierson, J., O'Brien, M., Misson, S. (2004) 'Who Pays for Sex and Why? An Analysis of Social and Motivational Factors Associated with Male Clients of Sex Worker', *Archives of Sexual Behaviour*, vol. 33, No. 4: 353–9.

Plant, M. (1990) 'Sex Work, Alcohol, Drugs and AIDS' in M. Plant (ed.), *AIDs, Drugs and Prostitution*. London: Routledge.

Plant, M. (1997) 'Alcohol, Drugs and Social Mileau' in G. Scambler and A. Scambler (eds.), *Rethinking Prostitution*. London: Routledge.

Plummer, K. (1975) *Sexual Stigma*. London: Routledge and Kegan Paul.

Plumridge, L. and Abel, G. (2001) 'A Segmented Sex Industry in New Zealand: Sexual and Personal Safety of Female Sex Workers', *Australian and New Zealand Journal of Public Health*, vol. 25, No. 1: 78–83.

Potter, K., Martin, J. and Roman, S. (1999) 'Early Development, Experiences of Female Sex Workers: A Comparative Study' in *Australian and New Zealand Journal of Psychiatry*, vol. 33: 935–40.

Potterat, J., Brewer, D., Muth, S., Rothenberg, R., Woodhouse, D., Muth J., Stites, H. and Brody S. (2004) 'Mortality in a Long-Term Open Cohort of Prostitute Women', *American Journal of Epidemiology*, vol. 159, No. 8: 778–85.

Potterat, J., Rothenberg, R. Muth, S., Darrow, W. and Phillips-Plummer, L. (1998) 'Pathways to Prostitution: The Chronology of Sexual and Drug Abuse Milestones' *Journal of Sex Research*, vol. 35, No. 4: 333–40.

Raphael, J., and Shapiro, D. (2002) *Sisters Speak Out: The Lives and Needs of Prostituted Women in Chicago*. Chicago: Centre for Impact Research.

Raphael, J., and Shapiro, D. (2004) 'Violence in Indoor and Outdoor Prostitution Venues' *Violence Against Women*, vol. 10, No. 2: 126–39.

Raymond, J. (2003) 'Ten Reasons For Not Legalising Prostitution' in M. Farley (ed.), *Prostitution, Trafficking and Traumatic Stress*. New York: The Haworth Press.

Raymond, J. (2004) 'Prostitution on Demand: Legalising the Buyers as Sexual Customers', *Violence Against Women*, vol. 10: 1156–86.

Rechard, D. (2005) *National Legislation on Prostitution and the Trafficking in Women and Children*. Policy Department C. Citizens Rights and Constitutional Affairs. European Parliament.

Red Thread (2006) *Rechten van Prostitutes*. Amsterdam: De Rode Draad.

Rekart, M. (2005) 'Sex Work Harm Reduction', *The Lancet*, vol. 366, Issue 9503: 2123–34.

Richardson, D. and May, H. (1999) 'Deserving Victims: Sexual Status and the Social Construction of Violence', *The Sociological Review*: 308–31.

Rickard, W. (2001) 'Been There, Seen It, Done It and Got the T-Shirt', *Feminist Review*, No. 67: 111–32.

Roberts, C. (2006) *No One Wants You: A Memoir of a Child Forced into Prostitution*. London: Merlin Publishing.

Roe, G. (2005) 'Harm Reduction as a Paradigm: Is Better Than Bad Good Enough?', *Critical Public Heath*, vol. 15, No. 3: 243–50.

Rosenberg, C. (1988) 'Disease and Social Order in America' in E. Fee and D. Fox (eds.), *AIDS: The Burden of History*. Berkeley: University of California Press.

Ryan, C. and Hall, M. (2001) *Sex Tourism*. London: Routledge.

Sagar, T. (2005) 'Street Watch: Concepts and Practice: Civilian Participation in Prostitution Control', *British Journal of Criminology*, vol. 45: 98–112.

Sagar, T. (2007) 'Tackling On-Street Sex Work: Anti-Social Behaviour Orders, Sex Workers and Inclusive Inter-Agency Initiatives', *Criminology and Criminal Justice*, vol. 7: 153–68.

Sampson, R. and Laub, J. (1993) *Crime in the Making; Pathways and Turning Points Through Life*. Cambridge, Mass: Harvard University Press.

Sampson, R. and Laub, J. (2003) 'Desistance From Crime Over the Life Course' in J. Mortimer and M. Shanahan (eds.), *Handbook of the Life Course*. New York: Kluwer.

Sampson, R. and Laub, J. (2003a) 'Life Course Desisters? Trajectories of Crime Among Delinquent Boys Followed to Age 70', *Criminology*, vol. 41, No. 3: 555–92.

Sanders, T. (2004) 'The Risks of Street Prostitution: Punters, Police and Protesters' *Urban Studies*, vol. 41, No. 9: 1703–17.

Sanders, T. (2005) *Sex Work: A Risky Business*. Collumpton: Willan.

Sanders, T. (2007) 'Becoming An Ex-Sex Worker: Making Transitions In and Out of a Deviant Career', *Feminist Criminology*, vol. 2, No. 1: 74–95.

Sanders, T. and Campbell, R. (2007) 'Designing Out Vulnerability, Building in Respect: Violence, Safety and Sex Work Policy', *British Journal of Sociology*, vol. 58, No. 1: 1–19.

Saner, E. (2007) 'You're Consenting to be Raped for Money'. *Guardian* 11th December.

Saphira, M. and Herbert, A. (2004) *Exiting Commercial Sexual Activity*. New Zealand: ECPAT.

Saphira, M. and Oliver, P. (2002) 'A Review of the Literature on Child Prostitution' in *Social Policy Journal of New Zealand*, Issue 19: 141–63.

Schur, E. (1965) *Crimes Without Victims: Deviant Behaviour and Public Policy*. Engelwood Cliffs NJ: Prentice Hall.

Scott, G. (1996) *The History of Prostitution*. London: Routledge.

Scott, J., Minichiello, V., Marino, R., Harvey, G., Jamieson, M. and Browne, J. (2005) 'Understanding the New Context of the Male Sex Work Industry', *Journal of Interpersonal Violence*, vol. 20, No. 3: 320–42.

Scott, S. and Skidmore, P. (2006) *Reducing the Risk: Barnardo's Support for Sexually Exploited Young People*. London: Barnardo's.

Scoular, J. (2004) 'The Subject of Prostitution', *Feminist Theory*, vol. 5, No. 3: 343–55.

Scoular, J. and O'Neill, M. (2007) 'Regulating Prostitution: Social inclusion, Responsibilisation, and the Politics of Prostitution Reform', *British Journal of Criminology online*.

Scoular, J., Pitcher., Campbell, R., Hubbard, P. and O'Neill, M. (2007) 'What is Anti-Social About Sex Work? The Changing Representation Prostitution's Incivility', *Community Safety Journal*, vol. 6, No. 1: 11–17.

Seal, N. and Salisbury, C. (2004) 'A Health Needs Assessment of Street-Based Prostitutes', *Journal of Public Health*, vol. 26, No. 2: 147–51.

Self, H. (2003) *Prostitution, Women and Misuse of the Law: The Fallen Daughters of Eve*. London: Frank Cross.

Sharpe, K. (1998) *Red Light, Blue light: Prostitutes, Punters and the Police.* Aldershot: Ashgate.

Shaw, I. and Butler, I. (1998) 'Understanding Young People and Prostitution: A Foundation for Practice?', *British Journal of Social Work*, vol. 28: 177–96.

Shrage, L. (1996) 'Prostitution and the Case for Decriminalisation', *Dissent* SEAS: 41–5.

Sibley, D. (1995) *Geographies of Exclusion.* London: Routledge.

Sides, J. (2006) 'Excavating the Postwar Sex District in San Francisco', *Journal of Urban History*, vol. 32, No. 3: 355–79

Silbert, H. and Pines, A. (1982) 'Entrance into Prostitution', *Youth and Society*, vol. 13, No. 4: 471–500.

Silbert, H. and Pines, A. (1982) 'Victimisation of Street Prostitutes', *Victimology*, vol. 7, Nos. 1–4: 122–33.

Simons, R. and Whitbeck, L. (1991) 'Sexual Abuse as a Precursor to Prostitution and Victimisation Among Adolescent and Homeless Women', *Journal of Family Issues*, vol. 12, No. 3: 361–79.

Skilbrei, M-L. (2001) 'The Rise and Fall of the Norwegian Massage Parlours' *Feminist Review*, No. 67: 63–76.

Social Exclusion Unit (2001) *Consultation on Young Runaways.* London: Social Exclusion Unit.

Socialstyrelsen (2004) *Prostitution in Sweden: Knowledge, Beliefs and Attitudes of Key Informants.* Available online on *www.socialstyrelsen.se.*

Solanki, A-R., Bateman, T., Boswell, G. and Hill, E. (2006) *Anti-Social Behaviour Orders.* Youth Justice Board.

Sontag, S. (1983) *Illness as a Metaphor.* Harmondsworth: Penguin.

Spangenberg, M. (2001) *Prostituted Youth in New York City: An Overview.* ECPAT-USA.

Sparks, R. (1981) 'Multiple Victimization: Evidence, Theory and Future Research', *Journal of Criminology Law and Criminology.* vol. 72, No. 2: 762–78.

Squires, P. and Stephen, D. (2005) *Rougher Justice: Anti-Social Behaviour and Young People.* Collumpton: Willan.

Sterk, C. and Elifson, K. (1990) *Drug-Related Violence and Street Prostitution.* Rockville, MD: NIDA monograph.

Strijbosch, M. (2006) 'Legalised Prostitution; A Dying Trade' www.radionetherlands.nl/currentaffairs/ned06103Imc.

Sullivan, B. (1995) 'Rethinking Prostitution' in B. Caine and T. Pringle (eds.), *Transitions: New Australian Feminisms.* Sydney: Allen and Unwin.

Sullivan, M. and Jeffreys, S. (2002) 'Legalisation: The Australian Experience', *Violence Against Women*, vol. 8, No. 9: 1140–48.

Surratt, H., Inciardi, J., Kurtz, S., and Kiley, M. (2004) 'Sex Work and Drug Use in a Subculture of Violence', *Culture and Delinquency*, vol. 50, No. 1: 43–59.

Svanstrom, Y. (2005) 'Through the Prism of Prostitution: Conceptions of Women and Sexuality in Sweden at Two Fins-de-Siecle', *Nordic Journal of Women's Studies*, vol. 13, No. 1: 48–58.

Svanstrom, Y. (2006) 'Prostitution in Sweden; Debates and Policies 1980–2004' in G. Gaugoli and N. Westmarland (eds.), *International Approaches to Prostitution.* Bristol: Policy Press.

Swann, S. (1998) 'A Model for Understanding Abuse Through Prostitution' in *Whose Daughter Next? Children Abused Through Prostitution*. London: Barnardo's.

Swann, S. and Balding, V. (2002) *Safeguarding Children Involved in Prostitution: Guidance Review*. London: Department of Health.

Swift, T. (2005) *Routes Out of Prostitution: Evaluation of the Intervention Team*. Glasgow: Social Inclusion Partnership, Glasgow City Council.

Terrell, N. (1997) 'Aggravated and Sexual Assaults Among Homeless Runaway Adolescents', *Youth and Society*, vol. 28, No. 3: 267–90.

Tonry, M. (1995) *Malign Neglect*. New York: Oxford University Press.

Tyler, K., Hoyt, D., and Whitbeck, L. (2000) 'The Effects of Early Sexual Abuse on Later Sexual Victimisation Among Female Homeless and Runaway Adolescents', *Journal of Interpersonal Violence*, vol. 15, No. 3: 235–50.

Tyler, K. and Johnson, K. (2006) 'Pathways In and Out of Substance Use Among Homeless Adults', *Journal of Adolescent Research*, vol. 21, No. 2: 133–57.

UKNSWP (2004) *Response to Paying the Price*. Manchester: United Kingdom Network of Sex Work Projects.

United Nations (2000) *Optional Protocol to the Convention on the Rights of the Child, on the Sale of Children, Child Prostitution and Child Pornography*. Geneva: UN.

Van Doorninck, M. and Campbell, R. (2006) 'Zoning and Street Sex Work: The Way Forward?' in R. Campbell and M. O'Neill (eds.), *Sex Work Now*. Collumpton: Willan.

Van Meeuwen, A., Swann, S., McNeish, D. and Edwards, S. (1998) *Whose Daughter Next? Children Abused Through Prostitution*. London: Barnardo's.

Visher, C. and Travis, J. (2003) 'Transitions from Prison to Community; Understanding Individual Pathways', *Annual Review of Sociology*, vol. 29: 89–113.

Wahab, S. (2006) 'Evaluating the Usefulness of a Prostitution Diversion Project', *Qualitative Social Work*, vol. 5: 67–92.

Walkowitz, J. (1977) 'The Making of an Outcast Group; Prostitutes and Working Women in Nineteenth Century Plymouth and Southampton' in M. Vicinus (ed.), *A Widening Sphere*. Indiana: Indiana University Press.

Walkowitz, J. (1980) *Prostitution in Victorian Society*. Cambridge: Cambridge University Press.

Ward, H. and Day, S. (1997) 'Health Care and Regulation: New Perspectives' in G. Scambler and A. Scambler (eds.), *Rethinking Criminology*. London: Routledge.

Ward, H. and Day, S. (2006) 'What Happens to Women Who Sell Sex? A Report of a Unique Occupational Cohort', *Sexually Transmitted Infections*, 82: 413–17.

Ward, H., Mercer, C., Wellings, K., Fenton, K., Erens, B., Copas, A., Johnson A. (2005) 'Who Pays For Sex? An Analysis of the Increasing Prevalence of Female Commercial Sex Contacts Among Men in Britain', *Sexually Transmitted Infections*. http://sti.bmj.com/cgi/content/abstract/81/6/467

Ward, L. and Gillan, A. (2006) 'Sex Slaves Trafficked to UK', *The Guardian*, May 30.

Weatherall, A. and Priestly, A. (2001) 'A Feminist Discourse Analysis of Sex Work' *Feminism and Psychology*, vol. 11, No. 3: 323–40.

Weber, A., Boivin, J-F., Blais, L., Haley, N. and Roy, Z. (2004) 'Predictors of Initiation Into Prostitution Among Female Street Youths', *Journal of Urban Health*, vol. 81, No. 4: 584–95.

Weeks, J. (2003) *Sexuality* (2nd edn). London: Routledge.

Weitzer, R. (1994) 'Community Groups vs Prostitutes', *Gauntlet*, vol 1: 121–4.

Weitzer, R. (2000) 'The Politics of Prostitution in America' in R. Weitzer (ed.), *Sex for Sale*. London: Routledge.

Weitzer, R. (2002) 'The Prostitutes Rights Campaign' in R. Weitzer (ed.), *Deviance and Social control*. New York: Mcgraw-Hill.

Weitzer, R. (2005) 'The Growing Moral Panic over Prostitution and Sex Trafficking', *The Criminologist*, vol. 5 September/October: 2–5.

Weitzer, R. (2005) 'New Directions in Research on Prostitution', *Crime, Law and Social Change*, vol. 43: 211–35.

West, D. (1992) *Male Prostitution*. London: Duckworth.

West, J. (2000) 'Prostitution: Collectives and the Policy of Regulation', *Gender, Work and Organisation*, vol. 7, No. 2: 106–18.

West, J. and Austin, T. (2005) 'Markets and Politics: Public and Private Relations in the Case of Prostitution', *The Sociological Review*, vol. 53 Supplement 2: 136–48.

Williamson, C. and Cluse-Tolar, T. (2002) 'Pimp Controlled Prostitution: Still an Integral Part of Street Life', *Violence Against Women*, vol. 5, No. 9: 1074–92.

Williamson, C. and Folaron, G. (2003) 'Understanding the Experiences of Street Level Prostitutes', *Qualitative Social Work*, vol. 2, No. 2: 271–87.

Wilson, J. and Kelling, G. (1982) 'Broken Windows: The Police and Neighbourhood Safety', *Atlantic Monthly*, March: 29–38.

Wolfenden, Lord (1957) *Report of the Committee on Homosexual Offences and Prostitution* Cmnd 257. London: HMSO.

Young, I. (1990) *Justice and The Politics of Difference*. New Jersey: Princeton University Press.

Young, J. (2001) 'Identity, Community and Social Exclusion' in R. Matthews and J. Pitts (eds.), *Crime, Disorder and Community Safety*. London: Routledge.

Young, J. (2007) *The Vertigo of Late Modernity*. London: Sage.

Zedner, L. (1997) 'Victims' in M. Maguire., R. Morgan. and R. Reiner (eds.), *The Oxford Handbook of Criminology* (2nd edn). Oxford: Oxford University Press.

Index